BEYOND THE REFLECTION

BEYOND THE REFLECTION

By Sahara

ISBN 1-58500-788-9

Cover photography by Dale Fahey, Chicago, IL

1stBooks – rev. 06/21/00

About the Book

While trying to think of what I could possibly write to encourage people to read "Beyond the Reflection", I remembered a letter a dear friend had written after reading my book for the first time. It brought me to tears and renewed my courage to publish...

"I must say, your book moved and inspired me beyond my wildest dreams. It filled me with a storm of emotions, lots of tears and nearly as many smiles... I feel your innocence and your torment, your strength and your weakness, your bliss and your sadness... As I journey at your side through a river of emotion and enlightened discovery... I witness your continuing evolution, I see you shed your painful cocoon and spread delicate wings, the splendorous beauty of your being... I cry, I love and I learn." -D. Berarducci

Beyond the Reflection is more like reading a diary than a book, the innermost pages of one's soul. Within it, you will experience what it is like to walk in another's shoes, feel another's world and struggles along the way, hopefully gaining more insight and understanding for your own. This book is meant to be a guide, a map for people of all ages, but especially young people reminding you that we all feel pain and we all are searching for love and acceptance.

Acknowledgement

I'd like to thank my parents for bringing me onto this planet, and my step-dad for choosing to raise me as his own. I want to thank my many, many teachers, some more obvious than others, some who have inspired me quietly, unknowingly. I want to thank all of the brave spiritual teachers who are speaking their stories and their truth in the world at this time, lighting the way for earth's children. I want to thank God, the fabric of All That Is, for the eternal patience, love and free-will that You have blessed me with. I could not be who I am today, without all of you.

This book is dedicated to all the youth everywhere who feel hopeless, separate, and alone. And to the ones we have lost because they felt this way. Peace Sierra, and to the others we will never know but never forget.

So here begins a journey in search of my innermost self and of why I have been born into this world. Recently I have gained a new awareness about myself and of the uniqueness that was mine all along, but was forgotten in the process of "growing up." I am truly lucky to have made this discovery so early in life because it has given me new hope for my future and on a larger scale, new hope for the future of this planet.

As children we are innocent and look upon the world with wonder and uncritical eyes. As we grow towards adulthood something happens that makes us forget how to experience life freshly and naively. Children grow up to be adults who wish to be children again. We lose our sense of mystery, imagination and openness in our everyday lives. We become the adults of this world who are responsible for raising and teaching children and yet we are the same people who are starting wars, neglecting the homeless, raising taxes and polluting the earth. So why has this endless cycle continued for centuries? I believe it is because in the process of life we lose touch with the Real person within ourselves. I don't believe that a baby coming from the womb is born evil. A baby Is pure innocence. I do believe that like the babies we all once were, humans Are inherently good at the core. Stephen Spielberg once said when talking about his movie "Schindler's List", "People are not born with hatred. They acquire it." What we judge to be evil results when our core or soul is layered with pain, disappointment, guilt, anger, shame and other dark emotions. If children are not allowed or encouraged to express and let go of these feelings we all experience, they continue to build and grow upon our core throughout life. Before long, we can no longer reach within ourselves past all of these layers of old emotion to find that inner person. We learn from a very young age to bury our pains and fears deep into the back of our minds where we think they will remain hidden. When something bad happens, we're taught to forget it and we put up a defense to never feel that hurt again.

Pretty soon we've built an armor of protection to keep us safe from life's bruises. These emotional "walls" that we build may feel like they are protecting our vulnerability, but at the same time they prevent us from being truly open to the world around us, from taking risks and from reaching into our own emotional depths.

Frequently we follow paths that our parents or society lead us to, forgetting the dreams we held so close to our hearts as children. Many become lost along the way and go in dangerous directions. As we grow into adulthood we may never feel truly fulfilled and even feel separate from others, but we don't know how to change or that there is even another option. Endless distractions and daily survival keeps us from ever finding out Who we are or why we've become that way. Most of our energy is spent coping instead of fulfilling our dreams. Over the years, this process becomes accepted as a part of life.

For ages, people have been searching for this sense of fulfillment. We have looked out across our lands, down into our seas and out into space. As a race we have grown intellectually and have made wonderful discoveries because of this search. But the time has come to stop reaching out and reach within. We are coming to a point in Earth's life where equilibrium must be restored. Our growing technology and world affairs need a spiritual balance. Our discoveries will mean nothing if we don't develop a conscious way of living on the planet we are now destroying. I feel that if people cannot find and be true to their own inner self, then we will never be true to each other or to this planet.

I see an exciting transformation occurring globally and people are awakening every day to a new sense of hope and purpose. We are searching for and finding meaning in everyday living again. I think that each human has a unique reason for being here, but too many of us become so disillusioned in everyday survival that we leave our Real Person undiscovered along with our true destiny. I see the misery and hopelessness in people's eyes everywhere I go and want to reach out to them. I want people to know there is another more fulfilling way to live life. The more people who are awakened and filled with a sense of destiny, the more it will spread and introduce the entire world with a new higher level of consciousness.

I feel a key to this outcome rests in the hands of our youth. But we are faced with a challenge. Today's youth are troubled with a future that seems to be growing ever more complicated and chaotic. Much of kids energy is spent in destructive ways instead of trying to better our future. Kids are rebelling more than ever and have few healthy outlets for self-expression. The recent massacre in Littleton, Colorado is an example of the burning need for young people to express their pain, their fears and frustrations. As Laurie Beth Jones, author of "Jesus CEO", states about this need for expression, "If we keep painting over graffiti left by gang members, we will never take the time to figure out what they are trying to say. What good is it to paint over feelings, anyway? Ultimately they will always bleed through." And bleed people did.

If kids had more outlets for self-expression, especially in school, I am willing to bet we'd see much less violence and rebellion. By providing them with constructive outlets, they will be more likely to grow up to be healthy, creative, motivated adults, retaining the optimism of youth. If the young are taught to believe they have a purpose and are encouraged to discover it, perhaps their untainted ideas can offer fresh new potential to our future. If we can learn to be honest with the children, treat them with respect and importance, and encourage them to be their full potential, then our future looks brightly promising. If we, the adults of this world now, can begin to look at the children as Our teachers, perhaps we may be inspired by their innocence to remember our own.

In the course of this book I will share some of my experiences as a young person searching for a more fulfilling way of living life than what has normally surrounded me. As I take you on my personal journey, I reveal experiences that were extremely painful to look at and deal with. What I now understand is that facing the seeming negative experiences in our lives is as important to self-discovery as accepting the good. Bringing light to these dark places allows healing, growth, freedom and brings you closer to finding out who you are. Letting go of these old emotional "layers" liberates you from the dead weight of your pain and brings you closer to your inner self, the You who you truly are. My writing this book is an example of just that, by expressing my greatest fears and errors I set them free and discover more about who I truly am. Hopefully, in the process, I will empower someone else to do the same. My purpose for sharing this information is to remind anyone, especially young adults, that you are not alone in your struggles. Even though growing up can seem confusing and unfair, there is light at the end of the tunnel. Our life challenges and mistakes help us to learn and grow and can push us harder to fulfill our dreams. I'm here to remind you that no matter what your outside circumstances are, keep looking for that special person inside. I encourage you to look at, own and love All parts of yourself. My greatest hope is that my naked honesty will inspire you to search beyond the reflection and into a deeper understanding of yourself. I wish for you the strength to reach through the walls that may be preventing you from finding that beautiful soul within. Know that who you are matters, and is worth searching for.

Clothes hide our naked bodies
like layers hide our souls
Peel them away
and you are left alone
bare
pure
A babe before the world
to gaze upon in wonder
One by one
people begin to undress
Off comes a shoe
a shirt
a dress
A pile of clothes
begins to grow
Rising higher and higher
towards the sky
As the last article is removed
a torch is lit
The mound flames high
So brightly
the people are nearly blinded
When the last ash settles
a smoky haze clears
Revealing a million naked souls
crying naked tears

INNOCENCE LOST

Childhood was an essential time of my life, as is everyone's. I was born into a wonderfully loving family which gave me a strong core. Being an only child, I learned an important lesson early on that spending time alone is not so bad and much needed for self-discovery. Alone time allowed my imagination plenty of space to create all sorts of wonderful places and games. I also learned to be my own best friend. I lived with my mom, step-dad, grandma and grandpa who all took turns spending time with me. Sometimes I thought of my real father who I'd never met, but was happy with the family I did have. I had never known anything different and so it was normal to accept how things were. I looked to the world around me and the people to be my teachers and my friends.

My earliest memories were those of a pure love of life. I could spend hours looking at rocks or staring up at the faces in the clouds or creating magical kingdoms out of snow piles. My connection with the earth was as strong as that with my family. With the turn of the seasons came an overwhelming excitement about what new changes Mother Nature would bring me. I loved collecting rocks as a little girl and sometimes my pockets would get so heavy by the end of the day, I would have to be carried home. I recall a memory as early back as 5 years old of being in the Wisconsin Dells with my mom and grandma. We had gone on the "Duck" which was a land-water vehicle. One of the stops we made was in a woodsy area where we watched natives dance and sing. I don't remember exactly what I saw, but I do recall feeling totally fascinated by the show. In years to come I developed an interest in anything associated with Native Americans whether it be fabric designs, music, history or camping in the woods. Every day became a fresh new adventure and I couldn't learn or discover enough. Life was a great mystery that I believed would reveal itself as I grew up.

For a long time I loved school and playtime. The other children became the brothers and sisters I didn't have that I always wished for. One thing I never understood was why some kids were treated differently than me. I thought we were all basically the same, except that some of our skin color was different, there were boys as well as girls or some kids celebrated different holidays. I never judged these differences, I just observed them. In fact, I didn't know what judgement was. Throughout all of my grade-school years, I was put into accelerated classes and was rewarded for being a healthy well-rounded child. But there were always those other kids who were teased, or played by themselves or were punished for not following the rules. I always felt sorry for these "underdogs" and usually made friends with them.

We moved around a lot due to my parents business growing, so I was constantly experiencing change and learning how to adapt easily. This was never difficult until I grew older and started wanting the stability that other families appeared to have and the comfort of fitting in. My first memory of really caring what other people had or what they thought of me was in seventh grade. We had moved again and I started junior high at a new school. It was very small and most of the kids had known each other for years. I wanted so badly to fit in and be liked which some of the popular girls made really difficult for me by spreading rumors that I was a snob when I was just incredibly shy. Eventually I made friends and fell in puppy love with Jon who had the most beautiful crystal blue eyes I'd ever seen. But popularity seemed to be costing me my individuality. One day during Social Studies the class was being exceptionally rowdy during the middle of a test review. Mr. Sanken threatened to skip the review which we needed to pass the test. After several warnings the class was still acting up and I was infuriated. Nobody messed with my grades. I raised my hand and Mr. Sanken begrudgingly called on me. I stood up and in my toughest voice (which was still pretty mousy) told the class that they were being totally disrespectful to the people who cared about their grades. I asked them to please be quiet so we wouldn't all fail. We finished the review in stunned silence. I got a C on my test and was teased mercilessly for weeks. From that point on I tried never to be too different again.

Around this time hit puberty and my glass encased world came shattering down. Because I was an only child and my family wanted to protect me, I was very sheltered from reality. Mostly I lived in my own imagination and romantic fantasies about life that I had read in books or seen on TV. There was always so much love around me when I was young and I had few bad memories or experiences to teach me about life. The shock of reality came when my grandpa who lived with us was diagnosed with lung cancer. This was my first experience with disease and death and I never really believed anything so horrible could happen to someone in my family. Because his illness was terminal, Grandpa chose to stay at home until his inevitable death. We set up a hospital bed and had at home nursing care for him. Knowing how painful it was for my grandma and mom, I tried to be strong and mature and not express the grief I was experiencing. We watched Grandpa deteriorate right before our eyes and then slip into a coma.

The night we felt he was dying a priest came to read prayers. We watched his body tremble and jerk in pain as the cancer devoured his insides. I remember wondering what this priest could possibly do to help a man who had abused his body with alcohol and cigarettes for 50 years? This was a devastating awakening to me because I realized for the first time that adults did not offer much protection to the realities of life. Also, religion no longer comforted me. I longed for my grandpa's arms which smelled of Old Spice and smoke and the protection I'd always felt as a child. Something within me knew those days were over. I awoke in the middle of the night with a start just in time to hear my mom say, "He's gone." We buried Grandpa on St. Patrick's Day which is ironic because it was his Irish love of drinking that helped kill him. Singing "Come Follow Me" for friends and family at his funeral was the only part of the ceremony that enabled me to express my feelings about his death.

In the midst of my grandpa's dying, other events were causing confusion in my life. My parents business was going bankrupt and they fought a lot, I was having problems with my friends at school, and my sexuality was awakening. It seemed as if all I could think about were boys and having them close to me. I was ashamed of these feelings since no one had ever told me they were normal. None of my friends seemed to be having these strong sexual feelings, or if they were they were too embarrassed to talk about them also. They had explained the cold physical facts about puberty and sex in school but had left out the part about these overpowering feelings. I'll never forget something my grandpa said to me during this time. Two of my guy friends had come over to the house to hang out. When I came inside for dinner my grandpa looked at me jokingly and said, "I saw what you were doing out there with those two boys. Swapping spit." So not only did no one explain to me about the birds and the bees, I was being teased for doing something wrong when I was innocent of anything but having male friends. Although I'm sure Grandpa meant no harm, this incident deeply affected me and I began hiding my feelings and relationships from my family.

5

JOURNAL ENTRY: MAY 30th, 1988

It's my 13th birthday and my parents and I went to one of our favorite places, Lake Geneva, WI. In less than an hour we were driving home after getting into a fight.

When we got back to our tiny house, I couldn't find any privacy with my mom, dad, grandma, grandpa and four dogs around. My room being in the middle of the house and the only way through to my parents and grandparents bedrooms, I had no where to go and be alone. So I walked down the steps, down the mile long gravel driveway and a few more miles to the church. Living in the country, the only neighbors I knew weren't home so St. Mary's was the next closest place to go.

I decided I was running away even though I had no money. When I got to the church, there was a pig roast going on and I was disgusted by the sight of a torched pig on a stick. I sat for what felt like hours in the same spot and not one person noticed me or that anything was wrong. I felt incredibly sorry for myself and pissed off at all the adults in the world.

The smell of roasting corn set my stomach growling and I realized how hungry I was. It was starting to get cold too. My determination to run away was weakening and I decided to plan a little better next time. Luckily, mom noticed I was missing and had been driving around looking for me. Less than halfway home, she picked me up just as it was starting to get dark. We drove around for over an hour and talked. We had one of the best conversations ever and she told me how she felt trapped too. She and dad were having problems but she couldn't leave him. She shared stories about how hard her childhood was and it was weird how parallel our lives were. By the time we got home, we felt so close, like we were all that we had in the world.

October 3, 1988

I remember how I felt the first day I attended this junior high. Everyone knew each other and was talking, and there I

*sat, by myself. As I walked down the hall to my first class, I felt
as if everyone was watching me. I dreaded going to lunch but
luckily some girls introduced themselves and invited me to sit by
them. This made me feel much better.*

*In my old school I had so many friends and I felt comfortable
there. Now that I've been here a while, I've met a lot of new
people that I really like but it's still not the same.*

My best friend at the time was a girl named Andy. To this
day I still miss our forgotten friendship. Andy had a brother who
I had a huge crush on and we used to say that if I ever married
him we'd be true sisters. One summer day he noticed me in a
different way and that night he introduced me into a whole new
world of ecstatic feelings. All of my fantasies of what it would
be like to go farther than kissing a boy proved to be simply
delicious.   Eventually these secret encounters lost me my
virginity. What I did not know then but understand now is that
this loss of innocence opened up doors to an insatiable hunger I
will attempt to fill for the rest of my life. I had exposed myself
to a new kind of fulfillment than anything I had experienced
before. It wasn't until this occurrence that I realized my blood
father's love was a gaping hole missing and being close with a
boy seemed to fill it. I wanted desperately to feel that wholeness
again.

CREATING WALLS

By this time I was in high school which were horribly confusing years. Freshman year I was what many might call the "model student." I tried to do everything I thought was the "right thing to do" to get approval from my family and peers. I enrolled in honors classes, joined the school choir, played on the tennis team, ran for student council, participated in other extracurricular activities and belonged to the "popular group." On the outside I appeared to be this ideal child but on the inside I was a pressure cooker about to explode. I was living with problems at home, burning with a newborn sexuality and trying to keep up the angelic surface image of myself that everyone seemed to expect. What intensified the situation even more was moving in the middle of it all and having to start a new high school. And not just a new school, our biggest competitor. I felt like an alien who couldn't fit in anywhere and constantly felt out of place. It seemed so awful that no one knew who I really was on the inside. Like so many young adults, I was afraid to express what was happening inside myself for fear that people wouldn't understand me or judge me. I went along with the crowd, creating the person I thought I should be instead of acting like the person I knew I was.

My whole life felt unreal and fake. I hated how petty my friends could be, I hated that I was caught up in the popularity game even though I hurt people, I hated being treated differently because I was pretty and smart, I hated that my family and teachers thought I was so wonderful and what I despised most of all was that I would always pretend everything was fine. My insides were burning in frustration and I longed for someone to explain this world of contradiction and confusion. I didn't ask anyone for help because I assumed the answer would be that this was all part of "growing up." The most alarming thing was that underneath all of these layers of negative feelings, I felt there

9

was a special person woven into a web of lies too tight to escape from.

CHINA
I once knew a little girl who believed
if she dug far enough into her sandbox
could dig right through hell and into China
where a mysterious land was.
This little girl loved the world around her
She believed in adults
She trusted their words
She didn't know hate or how to hurt.
As her body began to grow
the little girl became lost somewhere inside
She no longer ran through fields
stars lost their magic at night
The world that once was her friend
turned its back
flowers became withered stems.
A woman emerged one shadowy night
and the little girl cried in the darkness
wanting the light.
As time passed on
the woman grew tired and old
Yet somewhere
in the depths of her silence
a tiny voice
whispered
the longings of her soul
But her ears had grown deaf
and couldn't quite hear
the intuitions of a dream
forgotten in fear.

The summer of 1990 something happened that confirmed all of the negative feelings I was experiencing. I was raped by a stranger at a party. It started out as what I thought was harmless flirting. He was drunk and locked me in a room where he pinned me down and pumped away until he was finished. He bit me on my thigh leaving a bruise that wouldn't let me forget that day for the next six weeks. Sex, which was something I thought was magical and beautiful was tinged with filth.

For over a year, I was too ashamed to speak about what had happened. As quickly as I could, I buried the memory. I felt that it was my fault somehow and that something like this could only happen to a "bad" person. On some level I knew I was responsible for attracting male attention to myself because I needed it so desperately. It wasn't until a friend of mine had a similar experience over a year later that I could talk of it. To this day, I am still working to heal the wound this left on my sexuality.

From that point on, my self-image continued on a downward spiral and I gave away sex like it wasn't part of my body. It just wasn't a sacred act anymore. If some stranger could take something so personal, then why couldn't anyone? I went from one boyfriend to the next hoping each time they could fulfill the emptiness inside me.

Bodies touch without feeling
words without sound
Afraid to look into
the icy blue mirrors of your soul
This emptiness is swallowing me into
its endless black mouth
Wanting to reach out in vain
to hearts that cannot be touched
Why can't you let me in?
Why can't I let you in?
Feeling the pain of an eternity

11

yet feeling nothing at all
I'm as heavy as a mountain
with the strength of a mouse
Can't anyone hear me?
I'M SICK OF SCREAMING SILENTLY!!

When I thought life couldn't get much worse, another horrible experience just about crushed me. On the night of our school's Halloween dance, I discovered that a friend of mine had been shot and killed. Sara's jealous ex-boyfriend was drunk and possibly on drugs when he went to try and get her back. No one knows if he went to her with the intention of murder or if he was just trying to scare her. Sara died instantaneously after being shot in the chest and Chas died a week later after shooting himself in the head.

Sara and Chas' death affected the entire school, community and was even on national news across the country. It made people everywhere pause from their daily routine and think about what makes kids so desperate?? How could a normal white middle class kid be driven to commit such an act?

What happened over the next few days felt like a miracle. Kids from all different grades and cliques, parents, teachers and faculty let their walls down. People began to communicate with and comfort one another. It was truly beautiful. Finally it seemed as if something good and true was emerging from this darkness. And then I think that people grew afraid of the vulnerability and lack of boundaries because within a week, everything had returned to normal. In fact, worse than normal. Order needed to be restored, "Life must go on." People began to compete about who knew Sara longer, or who had the funnier story to tell about her or who had the inside scoop about Chas' breakdown. I had only known Sara for a year and was made to feel like I had less grieving rights than others. She had been one of the first people to give me a chance at my new school and took me under her wing. And now she was gone.

I was sickened to the point that my grades drastically dropped, I got into an obsessive relationship with the school bad-boy, I began sleeping all the time and many nights I'd lock my door and think about suicide.

November 20, 1990
I remember you
So cute, so charming
That big cheshire grin
so captivating, so darling
The way you used to flip your hair
Or wave hand expressions in the air
All of those stupid words that only you could use
Like yak and geek I was always amused
You will never know how much I cared
Only in my thoughts
are those special moments shared
As time moves along
I find it harder to picture you in my mind
and easier to remember
all of those insignificant times
It's so hard to accept that you're gone
and that you left without saying good-bye
I sit here writing this useless poem
Wondering
Why???

Just to add a little tension breaker I'd like to say that not all of life was negative throughout these years. I did enjoy many fun friendships and relationships. I'm sure I partied a little too much to escape reality but I guess that is the only way I knew how to cope at the time. As long as I'm taking a little breather

I'd like to thank everyone and anyone who has come into my life if even for a brief encounter. And I'd also like to say I'm sorry to anyone I may have hurt in my learning process. I've learned so much from everyone which has allowed me to grow as a person. I am so grateful to you all. (Sorry, back to the depressing stuff.)

Several times I had feared pregnancy, and one fall afternoon my biggest fear came true. Watching in disbelief the test turned pink for pregnant. Dazed, I sat as the horror of this reality grew into an insurmountable nightmare. For the next two months I denied to myself the test results. To avoid dealing with my pregnancy I partied every weekend. One night I was visiting a friend away at college and left the party we were at early feeling drunk and sick. I was laying in bed when I felt a wetness between my legs and ran excitedly to the bathroom thinking my period had finally come. I sat on the toilet for what felt like forever, beginning to get worried because the blood would not stop. I had miscarried the life inside me.

When I looked in the mirror all I could see was ugliness. I thought that by changing my surface image I would feel better inside. So I constantly bought new clothes, cut off all my hair, went to the tanning spa and became obsessed with my eating habits and working out. I even began volunteering at the local hospital so that I felt my life had some meaning again. This depression lasted the rest of high school. The amazing thing was, no one even knew how deeply I was suffering. Not even my parents. I had become an expert at hiding everything inside behind walls and painting the picture of perfection on the outside. The few times I tried to reach out for help no one took me seriously because I appeared fine. I had proven myself to be a survivor who didn't need help and always pulled through. Feeling sorry for myself became my new theme and I could not get out of the rut I was in.

"And when you're in a slump, you're not in for much fun Unslumping yourself is not easily done. You will come to a

14

place where the streets are not marked. Some windows are lighted, but mostly they're darked. A place you could sprain both your elbow and chin! Do you dare stay out? Do you dare go in?

How much can you lose? How much can you win? And if you do go in should you turn left or right... Or right and three quarters? Or maybe not quite? Or go around back and sneak in from behind? Simple it's not, I'm afraid you will find, for a mind-maker-upper to make up his mind."

Oh, The Places You'll Go by Dr. Seuss

NOWHERE TO TURN

During this time of my life, I did not see any options for help. I was terrified of losing the respect of my family and peers and so I couldn't go to them. I didn't know who to turn to and so I found ways of coping myself. Luckily, I found a few essential people and places that affected me so positively because they offered a healthy way to express myself and escape from everyday life. Throughout high school I took art classes every semester. The art room made the rest of the world temporarily disappear. It was the only place I was able to quietly express what I was feeling without having to tell anyone anything. This special room became a place of freedom. And humor thanks to one of my incredible teachers Mr. Seaburger.

I also had a love for performing and went to an acting workshop in New York the summer before my senior year. In that one week I learned more about myself and life than I had in four years of high school. I glimpsed a new way of living that was entirely more real and fulfilling than the life that was slowly killing me. The workshop was all about expressing and discovering and accepting yourself. Oh, and it was about taking emotional risks too. The adults there treated us with discipline And respect. They didn't take our problems lightly and really cared about how we felt. It was discovered that many of the teens had eating disorders and they received special counseling. All the kids were put on a low sugar diet and given vitamin C which I hated at first, but by the end of the workshop I felt much healthier and less tired during the day. We were kept so busy and stimulated and we were also having fun, so there was very little time to get into trouble.

These simple things that require no textbooks were not encouraged in school as part of the curriculum. Most forms of expression were seen as rebellious or too many boundaries were attached to the freedoms we were granted. In fact, many schools are trying to cut programs and extra-curricular activities that do allow kids to have fun and express themselves.

August 18, 1992
Today was very, very, very long. I memorized my monologue for the showcase in NY but it still needs lots of work.
We had a campfire tonight and I started feeling really lonely. I'm just not like the other girls here, not as outgoing I guess.
*

Now I'm back at the cabin and everyone cheered me up. I guess they do like me. I still miss my boyfriend though.

August 21, 1992
Today was the most incredible day! I was awake before wake-up and ready to start. Tracy is the greatest actress I've ever met. During class she did her own five minute version of the Wizard of Oz that she'd performed at a state contest. It was amazing and inspired me to keep working on my own acting.
I had my showcase run-through in front of the whole group tonight. I was so scared I could hardly eat dinner. But I made it through, and oh what a rush!! Being on that stage was the greatest experience of my whole life!

What parents and teachers need to understand is that children desperately need to express themselves, they need to be heard, they need to be taken seriously by adults. Otherwise all of these unexpressed feelings are buried and eventually manifest in destructive ways. I think many adults have become so detached from their own childhood, filed them way back in the closet of their minds that they've forgotten how to relate to kids. Many adults demand respect or feel they must be authority figures and set standards. But children and young adults are extremely perceptive and sense the adults confusion in their own lives. Because they may not yet have the vocabulary to put words to their knowing, they grow resentful and don't understand why the "grown up" way is imposed upon them when the "rules" are rarely followed in the adult world. How can they be expected to follow rules when their very teachers aren't "walking their talk?" The young no longer accept the brush off statement; "I'm the adult and I say so." If children don't have the freedom and supportive guidance to discover who they truly are, they will only use their expressive energies in negative ways instead of productively. In the attempt to conform, control, keep the truth from or pressure kids to "do the right thing," they are being pushed towards rebellion or trying to live up to incredulous standards. I tried desperately to fit in and to follow a path that only led me to hopelessness. Luckily, my experience with the acting workshop had planted a seed of hope within me. Maybe it was possible to live another way, finding the happiness and freedom I had felt as a child.

I'd also like to remind kids that their parents are still learning and growing too. The learning process continues throughout all of life. Most parents love their children so much and truly believe that they are doing what is best. They don't want to see their kids make the same mistakes they felt they made. And our parents only have the experience of how their parents did things which in many cases wasn't a great job. And even if most moms and dads won't admit it, they make up how to parent as they go along, there is no instruction book. If both kids and parents could give each other a break from time to time, make compromises, open the communication lines or seek counseling if they don't know how, then perhaps growing up would be less turbulent for both sides.

I can only imagine how hard it must be for kids growing up without parents or positive role models. My childhood was very loving and yet I was still so lost for so long. No wonder why gangs become like the families the kids don't have. Most of those tough kids probably never received much love or nurturing and so they give back to the world only what they were taught. Usually survival of the fittest. A most cold unloving existence.

19

Which reminds me of a very sweet movie, "Ever After," which is based on the original Cinderella story. Drew Barrymore playing the peasant girl quotes Thomas Moore, Utopia to the prince, "If you suffer your people to be ill-educated and their manners corrupted from infancy, and then punish them for those crimes to which their first education disposed them, what else is to be concluded sire, but that you first make thieves and then punish them?"

December 5, 1992

The tiger caught me in his enormous paw, his razor sharp claws closing around me like steel prison bars. He raised me to his mouth and carefully popped me inside, during which, I was unbelievably calm. There was something comforting about his mouth, the way my body rolled around as if he were tasting an expensive wine. It was odd to me that he hadn't eaten me in one hungry bite, but rather, prolonged his pleasure, and mine. I lay silently, unresisting this warm cavern, awaiting my inevitable end. Most unexpectedly, the tiger opened his mouth and let me free. His only words were, "Go, you are too fine a catch for me." I hesitated to leave the warmth and comfort of the beast and looked at him expectantly. As I stared into his deep black eyes, I saw a sadness that will forever chill my heart. Reluctantly, I turned away and walked home in the cold, foggy night.

Waking up with a start, I felt my cat laying on my chest. He awoke with a gentle sigh and licked my hand with his sandpaper tongue. He looked at me almost knowingly and I wondered if we had the same dream.

COLD SEAT
Walking down
noisy halls
littered with paper and shallow talk
I spin the right numbers

to my private space
in this place of dreaded time
I've tried to fit in
I've done everything
I thought I was supposed to
and yet I'm still walking alone
to my next class
thankful to slither into the safety of my desk
Daydreaming behind the "good student's eyes"
I imagine a place
where people are kind and welcoming
a place where I fit in
The bell rings and I repeat the usual routine
counting the minutes
until I'm out of the swarm
and into another cold seat

Senior year, I returned with a little better attitude about the future and a burning desire to graduate. Taking an advanced placement English class not only helped get me through the year, it opened me up to a whole new way of being educated. I had always felt freedom in art class, but rarely in academic classes. Mr. Greenfield enabled me to look at English in an entirely new and exciting way. He taught us about symbolism which brought reading to a whole new level. He encouraged us to write about our own opinions and ideas. A teacher who finally wanted us to think for ourselves and hear our opinions! Somehow he managed to fulfill his school requirements as a teacher while still giving us plenty of freedom with our work. He shared his knowledge with us instead of lecturing at us. Mr. Greenfield did not just grade papers, he'd offer suggestions and help during his free time. And the things we were reading and understanding were about life! Wonderfully real things about life that no one else dared teach us. We held heated discussions about love and loss, existentialism, politics, religion, homosexuality, spirituality and many other real-life things.

And every so often, he would bring in his guitar and play while we would sit on the tops of our desks or lay on the floor. A peacefulness would overtake the room while we would all sing together the songs we knew or listen contentedly to those beyond our time.

I graduated Republicanville High School in June of 1993 with mixed feelings of regret and sadness about the past and excitement and anxiety for the future. The idea of a new start was appealing to me and I planned to make great changes in my life. A new freedom awaited that I hoped would ease my unhappiness.

> *So it's a new start*
> *bought a new life*
> *Packed your bags*
> *headed out in the night*
> *Put as many miles as you could*
> *between you and the ugly past*
> *So why can't you outrun the lingering ghosts?*
> *They seem to follow*
> *no matter how far you go*
> *Little outlaw girl*
> *when will you learn?*
> *No train can take you away*
> *from your own unhealed burns*
> *The darkness lies in the pit*
> *of your own heart*
> *Never will you truly*
> *get a new start*
> *Just take a look*
> *at what has been done*
> *Is it really so bad you must endlessly run?*
> *And whose judgement matters anyway?*

Only you have the power
to decide what's okay
Look at the imperfect world around you
See its flaws
And know you hold the power of redemption
within your spirits walls

FINDING ESCAPE

Freshman year fulfilled all of my expectations, and then some. Finally a new kind of freedom presented itself to me. The self-imposed noose around my neck seemed to loosen with my parents so far away. The largeness of the university allowed me to feel lost in the crowd and less pressure to be the best. No one really knew who I was or about my past. It felt so incredible to have a chance to start over.

I was paired up with a great roomate, Laura, and soon made lots of new friends who cared nothing of the old me. I'll never forget one afternoon, me, Laura and two of my other new friends who lived on our floor, ditched classes and hung out in the dorms in our pj's all day. We told secrets and shared so much, like kids again and felt so close by the end of the day. For the first time in a while, I felt that I had friends who really valued and respected me.

A few months into the year, Laura and I grew bored with the dorms and decided to "rush" a sorority. When I sat down in the auditorium with the hundreds of other girls to pick our final choice, I remember feeling so confused. I had narrowed it down to two sororities. The major difference between the two being that one was a "popular" pretty girl sorority and the other, still a good house but much more down to earth. As silly as it seems now, this was a huge decision for me because I so badly wanted to be happy and make the right choice. I did not want to go through the competitive high school games again and yet my ego wanted to be in the "best" house. After much thought I decided that "best" for me meant being in a sorority house that I could feel comfortable walking around with no make-up in my sweats. Being one of the last girls left, I checked the box and left, hoping I had made the right decision.

Pledging my house was a lot of work and a lot of fun. I was elected my pledge class president which was a great honor for me. When pledging was over and I had gotten to know the other girls, I was teased for taking the job a little too seriously. I just wanted so badly to become a new, better person that everything I did was to the best of my ability.

I joined the Black Student Caucus for awhile hoping to better understand the racial prejudice on campus and maybe be a small part in changing it. I have always felt much grief around our painful history with African Americans. Poets like Langston Hughes, Maya Angelou, books like Roots and Malcom X and movies such as the Color Purple and Mississippi Burning have inspired me to want to make a difference.

After several meetings of feeling unwanted and being one of two white people in the group, I reluctantly stopped going to the meetings. At the time I was frustrated by the rejection when I was just trying to be helpful. All of my schools growing up had been predominantly white and I'd never experienced having many black or ethnic friends. I even almost got beat up one afternoon on the elevator for saying "excuse me" to a black student which hurt me more emotionally than anything. Now I'm grateful for these incidents because I got to experience reverse discrimination and understand the disharmony a little better. I hoped for a day when all people see each other as one large human family.

Dark bittersweet skin
and midnight eyes
You are so beautiful
against the pale sky.
Why do you look at me
like I'm a stranger?
Our ancestors past
shouldn't fill you with anger at me
All I want
is to be free to love you.

That first year I handled my freedom pretty well. I went to endless sorority and fraternity functions, partied, went to most of my classes and managed to get good grades. I also fell completely in love for the first time. It was the first truly healthy relationship I had been in since my rape and I will love Anthony for that always. He gave purity back to love and sex for me and being with him made me feel whole. I can still remember the way he'd look at me with the most adoring, loving puppy dog eyes. He could also make me laugh like nobody else could. Anthony gave me a new belief in not only relationships but friendships also.

When we found out that he could not come back to school the next year, I think we both feared it was over. One of the saddest days of my life was the night we sat in his car in front of my sorority house and broke up. He handed me back my gold chain that he had worn for a year. I had never seen Anthony cry before and hated that I was the reason for his tears. Some old part of me just could not let him love me anymore. I wanted to go to fraternity dances with other guys, date and have the fun it appeared that all of my single friends were having. The whole situation didn't make sense to me. I didn't make sense to me.

Without Anthony with me all the time that longing and emptiness crept into my soul again. I wasn't finding the same completeness with other guys that I had felt with Anthony. The old me seemed to be creeping out of nowhere and I did not know how to deal with it. So I partied more. This time my escapes turned into truly destructive behavior. I had always loved to party because it gave me the temporary freedom to let go, but it soon turned into a curiosity and then needed escape with drugs.

GEMINI GIRL
Gemini girl
make up your mind
Does it taste sweet or sour?

27

Do you want it
or not?
The chase always seems better
than what you have got
You walk a fine line
between good and evil
Maybe your split twin
forfeits you from either
Perhaps Yin and Yang
Will call a truce someday
settling on
a warm shade of gray
But until then
the battle continues
Always losing to win
and winning to lose

My friends and I began experimenting. Some drugs had been around me in high school but I was too afraid to try anything except pot. We started out just getting high all the time which eventually led to a desire for something more powerful. Before long, we were doing acid, mushrooms, ecstasy, crystal meth, coke, "G" and others. Drugs became a part of our lifestyle and everything from the way we dressed, our music and even going to class revolved around our partying. I can remember hearing a new song or seeing a movie preview and getting excited to experience it on drugs. For my eyes and body to have experienced psychedelic pleasure was amazing to me. I had glimpsed other worlds that I thought held the mystery I longed for. Certain drugs, like ecstasy, bonded my friends and I like nothing else I've ever experienced. All inhibition and judgment were removed and I felt so much love for the friends around me. When we "X'd" we would brush each others hair, give hand or back massages or rub ice on one another. Things you just didn't do with people other than your boyfriend or girlfriend usually. It was so much fun and so loving- I'd never experienced anything like it in my normal world.

The amazing part was, that once you became a part of the druggie crowd you saw how many kids were doing them. To many, pot had become equivalent to drinking alcohol and ecstasy had become an every weekend event. Many kids I knew were what are referred to as "garbage heads"- kids who would try anything, mix anything in search of the perfect high. If you didn't have the money to play, someone else always did. We encouraged each other to do new drugs and pulled many new people into the "fun." For a while, life was exciting and mysterious. My feelings of insecurity were replaced with cool certainty because my friends and I did what other girls were afraid to do. Even at the expense of my health and my mind.

Freddie Jones Band 1994

Tonight we're in
a funhouse world
Look at the night sky
It's beginning to swirl
Comical faces stare as we dance by
Flowers for hair
Dreams in my eyes
Where can you find a crazier high?

I remember camping out before my first "dead" show and being surrounded by a bunch of strangers who became familiar friends by the end of the night. It was like this neat little non-judgmental community where anything that didn't disturb the peacefulness was acceptable. Everyone shared their smoke, their music and I even borrowed a tent which I'd forgotten to bring. My friends Flower and Shawn and I sat in a circle with our stranger-friends around a campfire. Flower brought her craft box with and did wraps in our hair. People played guitars, drummed and the blazing fire warmed my comfortably numb body. To me, this setting was like a dream come true. I wanted so badly to believe I had found the fulfillment I was searching for that I was able to overlook the fact that everyone appeared so happy because they were on alcohol and drugs. And that come daylight, reality would soon wrap its ever-tightening grip around me.

In support of "deadheads" or "hippies" I give them the credit they deserve. They have the right idea about peace and community. I heard a story about a guy we knew losing his dog at a Grateful Dead show. A few months down the tour this guy saw his dog at another show and when he called it by name, the dog came. When he explained what had happened to the new owners, they returned the dog, no questions asked. I truly met some of the most interesting, helpful and down to earth people at the shows. I just wish they would eventually let go of the drugs and see that their tendency is an escapist one. I know from experience how much easier it is to hide from society than confront it or change it. Jerry Garcia's death was a huge awakening to his followers like when Forrest Gump stopped running and one of his groupies asked, "What do we do now?" I truly hope his death helped people to see that the high life eventually comes to an end.

31

DRUG LOVIN' WIFE
Where'd your mind go
Was it on a magic carpet ride
or playin' in the snow?
Looking in your eyes
used to say it all
Now all that's there
is a glossy eyed stare
Can't be your lover
can't be in your life
All you need is a
drug lovin' wife
Legs entwined
while sweet words were spoken
Must have been all that
shit we were smokin
Sitting here
so far away
Wishing I could
save you someday
Misery loves company
That's all that we were
Just two lost souls
snuggling in our black hole
Can't be your lover
Can't be in your life
All you need is a
drug lovin' wife

July 27, 1995
I remember the first time I went "clubbing" in Chicago. I borrowed an ID and easily got into the club. Everyone standing in line outside looked different. Different than the strangers I went to school with everyday who made me feel like an outsider.

33

I was intrigued by the way they were dressed, mostly in black with strange hair, nose-rings, Doc Martens and a cigarette in hand. Immediately I felt more comfortable with who I was because I was surrounded by, what my high-school friends used to call "freaks." Meaning, people who were different from the norm, who seemed to thrive on their strangeness.

As I entered the darkness of the club, I was immediately lured by the music. It seemed to be erotically pulling me forward into its pounding rhythms. Already I wanted to know more about this deliciously strange underground world. I felt like a virgin again within it. Every person I saw had an air of danger and excitement and a distaste for the normal. The dance floor felt like I was part of some primal culture whose people were uninhibited. This scene seemed to feed upon my increasing dislike for the everyday world with its everyday people. I fell dangerously in love with this dark club, the dark people and especially the dark music that seeped into my veins and made me feel high.

Little did I know that there was more to the package than my eyes saw that night. I did not know that this mysterious lifestyle attracted so many unhappy kids like myself. People who did not think much about the future, people whose only thoughts were in the moment they did a line in the bathroom stall.

TEMPTER OF THE NIGHT
Dancing
fluid-like
my body is melting
into the floor
Waves of energy
shock my spine
Pulsing
Beating
Pounding
Absorbing

I am the sound
that makes you feel hungry
Wanting to lose all control
Slowly you forget yourself
spinning into the light
Weightless
Floating
Flying
Feeling
I am tempting you
into this night
Come with me
out of reality
I can take you
away from this world
Hear the music
You know it is
Calling
Pleading
Enticing
Luring
your soul to abandon itself
Just one night
I'll take you
away from the pain
Fearless
Daring
Erotic
Darkness
I become lost in you
Tempter of the Night
Confused
Lost
Angry
Helpless

Don't leave me this way
The daylight is hurting my eyes
Blinded
Afraid
Tired
Empty
I live in the shadows
worshipping
this dark god of the night

Clubbing was yet another reason why the drug scene was so addictive. The music and the lights and the hypnotic, sensual music were enough to make you feel high. Unless you were a druggie and you wanted it to be even More amazing. Clubs and raves, for the most part, are a place where kids feel free. Whatever free means to each person. To some it means having a place to dress crazy, to others it means having sex in public, and to kids like me, they were a place to do drugs, dance and bliss out. I never felt weird or unwanted at these parties because there was always someone stranger than me and yet I didn't judge them for being different. This may seem bizarre to a mainstream person- why would anyone Want to look or act weird?? I think some of it is because kids self-expression is so repressed that when it finally does come out sometimes it is in very extreme ways. Maybe we are rebelling against a world that is boring us to death with its rules and normalcy. Maybe my generation expresses what everyone else just Thinks about.

Before long, the short term escape drugs brought wasn't worth the long term damage it was bringing to my body. The last time I dropped acid over twelve hours had passed and my trip was supposed to be over but my mind was spinning so fast that I couldn't grasp a single thought. I lay paralyzed by fear and when my mind slowed down all I could think were dark, horrible things. Before finally dozing off, I remember thinking, what if my mind never snaps out of this? I can't even describe how

36

frightening the thought was. I began having anxiety attacks and the increasing feeling of despair returned when I was sober. So I lived for the weekends when I could really party. Even though I knew the drugs were destroying my mind and my willpower, I still continued to party because I felt trapped somehow. I had never found a niche like this before- a place where everyone I hung with was non-judgmental and just looking to have fun. Nothing else really mattered but my friends and our lifestyle. Life had rarely offered me anything better than what I had- I put up with my low's because the high's were always fun.

In my attempt to gain independence and freedom from all that hurt me, the actions I chose produced exactly the opposite results. I was trapped in my own escapes. I hurt myself and my loved ones deeply. I had lost all my sense of hope, purpose and motivation in life.

ICE DRAGON

Ice Dragon
May I board your
cold wings tonight?
Fly me away
from the violent waters
High above this painful life
I want to go
where the world is numb
Color is dead
No reason to run
Feelings are creatures
long extinct
Here nothing matters
No memories
Only emptiness lies within
the castle walls
The princess no longer

waits in the tower
Her knight has forgotten
how to shine his armor
Passionless dead world of mine
Never will I return
to the place where emotion lies
Where happiness embraces
its Gemini twin pain
I want to forever live
in the Ice Dragon's world
Where the only law
is to feel nothing again

Luckily for me, I soon realized that what we were doing was not mysterious or glamorous and would never be fulfilling. It was a deathtrap. My eyes were forced open to the fact that we were not invincible when a few more people in my life died. A friend from high school fell down an elevator shaft and died due to drinking. A guy who I'd gone out with a few times had a heart attack after doing crack while on steroids. And most recently, I learned that a friend was killed while driving drunk. Countless other people I know have O.D. and ended up in the hospital, been arrested and have committed suicide. Sadly, I have witnessed some of the strongest, smartest people get sucked into this lifestyle and I'm afraid it will take years before they escape from it or die from it.

Sitting here alone
My private sanctuary has become
the reflection of my soul
Sound of music
is my only peace
A world once filled
with mystery
Is slipping

slipping
away...
When years pass on
what will fill the empty space
that is my fear??
Running thoughts
swirling
twirling
escaping me
Never to be expressed
Wasted and lost
to the darkness of
my temptations

SOMETHING'S MISSING

I think why drugs have become so popular with kids, is not only for the escape, but because of the sense of mystery and spirituality they provide. Drugs take you to worlds beyond the mundane everyday experience. People who do drugs are usually yearning for something more and feel that something is missing in life. Isn't that partly what spirituality is about? This may be difficult for someone who has never experienced drugs before to understand. Every time I tried a new drug it was a very personal, spiritual experience and not just a means to get messed up.

Let me just clarify here that when I speak of spirituality I'm not referring to religion; to me there is a distinct difference. I view religion as an organized way of worshipping an outer god whereas being spiritual is a very individual way of connecting with your own inner self. There is no need to join a church and pay money to be spiritual. You can light candles, spend time in nature, listen to music, create art or countless other ways. However you can connect with and express your inner self is spiritual.

Somehow, drugs enabled me to tap into a very primal and expressive part of myself that I normally would not let out in front of others. I felt like a child again who could do, say or see anything. I thought I had found not only myself in drugs but my god also. I felt uninhibited and a deep appreciation for life and the people around me. I had never experienced the closeness that I did with my friends who partied with me. Many of them had messed up childhoods and we knew each other's good and bad points. We were there in the "high" moments and also there in the lows when someone was puking or just depressed. It wasn't all just about getting messed up- it was about feeling like you were loved and belonged somewhere. For a very short time the drugs softened life so that I could finally find a place within it. That euphoria only lasted a short while until the drugs began

41

deteriorating my nervous system, emptying my mind and causing emotional turmoil. The joy and escape they provided for a time, only brought me deeper into my feelings of emptiness in the end.

I do think certain drugs have a purpose of showing us the existence of other realities or as a way of tapping into other parts of our brain. I also know that drugs are not the only way or the safest way to do so. There are many teachers and workshops available for people who are interested in accessing other dimensions in a natural way. Yoga, shaman work, energy healing, crystals and many other options are available for this purpose. In fact, if you or someone you know is trying to quit drugs but is still wanting to experience the mystical in their lives, I highly recommend checking out these alternatives. I have had incredible experiences in meditation similar to my drug experiences. It is a much safer and long-lasting way to feel high. Most cities have at least one alternative bookstore where you can find out more information about local options. If not, major bookstores have a New Age section loaded with all sorts of wonderful books.

One of the biggest problems in the war against drugs is first of all, it's a war. You cannot solve problems with fear, blame and anger as your driving force. Only our desire to understand and our willingness to have compassion are going to make permanent changes. If I had known that my parents and the rest of society would not have judged and blamed me for having experimented with drugs, then perhaps I would have reached out and asked for help. Maybe I would not have had to hit rock bottom and go through my recovery process alone. Maybe everyone could have learned from my experience. Which is why I share this information with you now. If I can help just one person to change their life then maybe they will make a difference in someone else's life and so on and so on.

Remember that commercial with the crazy haired girl dancing around singing the catchy little jingle, "Users are losers and losers are users. So don't use drugs, don't use drugs." That ad campaign certainly does no good for kids like me who aren't losers but happened to really need some help and I'm being told I'm a loser for being where I'm at! And I happened to be where I was, not because I was a problem child or lacked love in my formative years, but because of a dilemma that has it's roots in All of society. People have drug and alcohol problems because they feel hopeless. It is a societal sickness and we cannot just forcefully kill the problem. We need to follow the problem to it's roots or it will just keep sprouting. Society is quick to blame messed up people for their "crimes" and yet we Allow the conditions that spark the crime in the first place.

Another problem is that the basic message is "don't do drugs." Just like alcohol, smoking, sex or any other thing minors aren't supposed to do, drugs are alluring because they are off limits. Teens especially, seem to always want what they can't have. When a person's right to choose is taken away, minor or not, you have taken away the "free will" that God intended for us. As I'm sure you're aware of, taking drugs for any length of time has built in consequences that no human has any control over. If an individual chooses to experiment with drugs for the experience, I feel they are being open-minded. If they abuse them and never find another alternative like meditation, then their punishment is already built in- they will experience the aftermath. I would rather see someone play around with alcohol and drugs for a short while in search of themselves, than many judgmental adults who just moderately drink away their pains their entire lives, most likely killing more brain cells than I ever did. (I'm not encouraging Either option.) More education about the harmful effects drugs have on our bodies combined with powerful movies and assemblies in school seem like a good place to start. Counselors who kids feel they can trust without getting busted are also necessary when their is already a problem. Also, if parents or family members are not willing to go through counseling and look at how they may have contributed to a child's interest in drugs, then they have no real right to stop the child. Blame and denial have no place in recovery.

The last major problem I see is that drugs, alcohol, smoking and sex have all been glamorized over the years. We hang posters and hold tributes to Elvis, Marilyn Monroe, Kurt Kobain, Jerry Garcia and others. TV and magazines have made being glamorous and beautiful a necessity to many humans and we spend billions each year to feel that way about ourselves. And when we don't feel glamorous enough, we do things like smoke or drink to give us a temporary high and illusion of beauty. We can begin change by not buying fashion magazines or watching TV stations that add to this destructiveness.

During much of high school, I dated our school bad-boy who was eventually kicked out before our senior year. I met Joe right after I started at my new school and we were friends for quite some time before we started dating. He was involved in sports every semester and weight-lifted almost every day. Behind Joe's tough exterior was a really good guy, but he had an "image" to uphold. He was one of the first people I was able to talk to about my rape with and of course he wanted to find the guy and kick his ass. I could hardly believe the first time he told me he loved me and I actually felt honored that he would be that vulnerable with me. After getting in too many fights, and being caught with chewing tobacco, he was eventually kicked off of sports for good. And that is when his downfall began. With too much free-time on his hands and frustration at not being able to play football or wrestle, Joe began to party more and more. Pretty soon he became a wake-n-baker and spent most of his time getting drunk and high and being fired from jobs. On our senior trip to Cancun, Joe went with some of his friends and of course he partied too hard. I spent one of our last nights there sitting up with him half the night as he vomited all over the place because he did acid, smoked pot and drank too much alcohol.

44

I'm not sure what happened to Joe, although I'm not sure I want to know. What is frustrating to me is that Joe was a good guy, an honor roll student in Jr. High and excellent in sports and yet, he turned out to be so screwed up. I feel our school and his parents failed him by just punishing him and not finding out why he was so rebellious and so in need of escape. When they took away his sports, they took with it his only healthy outlet for aggression. For awhile, I was able to get through his walls and get him to share his feelings until he got too numbed out on alcohol and drugs. Then it was beyond my control.

Violence has become such a natural part of our culture, all you have to do is flip on tv for news or an action film, and yet we punish our kids when their behavior is aggressive. I've read several times now about people placing blame on the movie industries because they are too violent. But they won't stop creating these films until we stop going to them. Industries make what the consumers demand.

Young Blood
Does danger excite you?
Does the vampire life
entice you?
Beware of this dream
It's emptier than
your harsh reality may seem
The pretty escapes may tempt you
but loneliness
will haunt you
Run while you are still free
Before your mind traps
and leaves you
An empty endless
wanderer
in a wasteland sea

At school I felt surrounded by darkness and my grandma was now slowly dying of Alzheimer's at home. I could no longer escape these things happening around me or the returning pain inside me. I napped much of the time and missed a lot of my classes. I lost all interest in my sorority and my duty on its Executive Board.

In the midst of this depression a strange thing happened. Inside my feelings of despair came a spark of hope that I could change what was happening to me. A nagging voice kept reminding me that this wasn't the person I was supposed to be! Something was missing but I didn't exactly know what, or how to get it.

My one true love growing up had been performing and I remembered the fulfillment I had felt at the acting workshop. So I enrolled in an acting class to see if I still had a performer in me. Part of the class requirement was to audition for scenes that the graduate students directed. After getting a leading role in one of the short plays I realized that acting was a great motivation because I enjoyed it so much. I really liked pretending not to be me too. I thought that maybe if I became absorbed in acting I wouldn't have time to get in trouble, so I decided to audition for the theater department. Also, I knew that I needed some sort of self-expression besides partying.

The night before my audition I could barely sleep. No one had even seen the monologue I had prepared. Just before leaving to audition for the director of the department, I had a panic attack and almost chickened out. I had to try my monologue out in front of someone. It was about a girl meeting her father for the first time. My roommate Dylan had just come home from class and so I performed for her. When I finished, I looked down at her sitting on the floor with tears in her eyes. She gave me a huge hug and with that, I had the confidence to go and audition. Three weeks later I had been accepted!

Paralyzed by fear
Who can you turn to
but yourself?
Same answers to those
nagging questions
Pain no one can hear
Drifting through the daydream
that is your life
Which path do you follow?
Is any way wrong or right?
Some days better
than others
Others darkness is blinding you
Please promise me
I'll find my way to truth

August 1, 1995
Are there ever times in your life when you feel like you've just begun to live? It's like an awakening when you find meaning in a song you've heard a hundred times or you hear a personal message in a great novel or maybe you've just fallen in love again. These are the feelings to remember when you can't see the light at the end of the tunnel.

The summer before my junior year, I began feeling weary of going back to school and having the strength to stay focused in an environment that I knew was so destructive. I was ready for a big change. I kept thinking about the acting workshop and how much it had helped me during high school. I decided that I wanted to go as a chaperone now that I was old enough. It had been three years since I'd spoken to the director of the workshop and was nervous to call him out of the blue. Finally as the summer neared its end, I got up the nerve to call. To my great surprise, not only did he need a chaperone, he needed a full-time assistant for the program in New York. Without hesitation, I packed my bags and left for this new adventure. I knew life had handed me yet another opportunity to try again.

Solitude has become a way of life
Staying true to myself the ultimate quest
Finding peace for my soul
a never ending journey
If I am aware of these things
then why do I so often fall down?
How am I capable of creating
so much pain and darkness?
Time spent in appreciation of
the poetry of life
While also picking up the pieces
of what has been lost
What is the better way to live?
In blindness and illusion
or this painful reality?

NEW BEGINNINGS

Working for the acting workshop was truly the beginning of a new way of living and being for me. The changes did not come easily though. I was used to cutting corners and having things come easy in my early life, so I didn't really understand what overcoming a challenge was. Many times when confronted, I gave up and walked away. I usually took the escape instead of facing my fears. Until now, I didn't know the sweet satisfaction of defeating obstacles until I had no choice at the workshop. New York was not home- it really was "make it or break it."

The few months I interned felt like rehab while I was there. I was not allowed to smoke and had to quit cold turkey. I had to rebuild my mind after the drugs and alcohol had weakened it. This happened slowly by eating healthy, taking vitamins and herbs as well as getting regular sleep. Like drugs had once done, the herbs and vitamins opened my mind again, only in a healthy way. My mental energy and clarity was unlike ever before. My hormones balanced out again lessening my mood swings and depression. I also realized for the first time that when I ate it wasn't just to fulfill hunger or cravings. The healthy foods I ate nourished my body and gave me the energy I needed to be productive. No wonder why fast food employees can be so grouchy - they are probably malnourished. For the first time in years I had energy again and didn't need an hour nap during the day. Because I felt healthy, I looked at life more positively and was open to more new things. Instead of feeling sorry for myself in times of loneliness I started reading, journaling regularly and writing poetry. I began taking acting classes in the city once a week that also helped me to express myself and get to know myself better.

September 9, 1995

This has got to be the perfect end to an incredible day. I met with some talent agents and managers at a workshop today and got promising feedback from all of them.

This seminar was so valuable for me professionally and personally. All of the positive feedback that I received not only gave me more confidence, but also was a reward, I feel, for taking the risk to come to NY. This whole day has been a positive reinforcement in myself and my dream. So there is a chance of someday soon being a professional actress in this city!

I'm flipping through cable and a public TV station is playing clips from dead shows as a tribute to Jerry. Summertime memories are flooding back; bittersweet memories of freedom and captivity. It's amazing that what seemed in the moment to be such an essential part of my life is now over and so distant from my future dreams. I will never forget this time of experimentation, crazy fun and deep sorrow. I know it has found a place in my soul that I will forever return to with longing. I only hope to find the same freedom within myself that I once found with alcohol and drugs. Until then, I feel there is every reason to search for meaning in what many times feels like a meaningless world.

September 16, 1995

Wow. I just experienced my first class with May at her studio outside of the acting workshop and it was out of this world. In a period of four hours, every person attending had some kind of breakthrough. In front of everyone I had to tell about something that deeply moved and upset me. I talked about how I once used to be with people- caring, complimentary, a true friend. And now I've built walls from being hurt or laughed at, shunned. I also told how things that I appreciated, others usually don't.

50

Photograph by Dale Fahey, Chicago

My feedback was, instead of being hurt by the person who doesn't perceive things how I do, to be happy just knowing that I can see something that they can't. And to only share feelings with people who will appreciate and accept my feelings.

October 2, 1995

What an invigorating class tonight's was! When I first got up in front of the class, my assignment was to have a temper tantrum. By the end of the tantrum I had completely lost control and was holding my breath, stomping, screaming, pleading and had that child-like feeling of not caring about consequences. What an emotional orgasm that was!

I then was told to go to each person, look into their eyes and tell them, "I'm just a little girl and I want my mommy." When I had to do that saying daddy, I began to cry. It was amazing the way those buried feelings crept up and out of me. I could have let go even more but my adult came and held my little girl back.

I then had to go around the room saying, "If you could see inside of me, you would see..." and then say whatever feeling that person aroused in me. When I got to May, I told her that she'd see someone who felt so much empathy sometimes that it hurt her. We really had a moment of understanding that I'll remember for quite some time.

My feedback was so encouraging. Bob told me that when I let go, I was amazing to watch and my eyes shone with intensity. Pat told me that when I looked at someone, they became my universe and he felt embraced by me at that moment. Helen said she really adored me and related to everything I said and felt we could be good friends. And Sharon, I'm not quite sure what happened between us tonight. I think she admitted to me that she was attracted to me. I'm not sure how I feel about that, other than a little surprised, but not really bothered by it. The only negative feedback I received was that I have a major perfectionist in me.

52

The realization dawned that I had been trapped in a sheltered way of life and thinking. So much of what I believed and did was not my own. I became this blank slate who had nothing of her past to believe in anymore. There was no one to think for me; no mom, no friends, no teachers, just me. And at times, I did feel so alone. It was truly scary to just walk away from my life even though I wasn't happy. But it seemed as if during those moments of aloness and quiet, I discovered strengths that I never knew existed. I learned that instead of falling deeper into my feelings of unhappiness, to let my pain motivate me to change. It was in those alone moments, I realized, that I had lost sight of a beautiful, talented little girl inside me.

November 10, 1995
So here I am in Grand Central Station sitting on the cold marble floor listening to a reggae singer. Bittersweet memories of the past are floating through my mind and I'm feeling very alone. The singer is doing his own version of Bob Marley's "No Woman No Cry" and he referred to Grand Central as the Carnegie Hall of subways. I'm sitting here with a handful of other lonely looking people and as the suits rush by, I wonder if the music touches them. The singer looks so small in contrast with the immense building and yet his beautifully sorrowful voice fills the entire room. Now he is trying to get his small audience to sing along together but every time he holds out the microphone he is responded with silence. He tells us that he's trying really hard to communicate with us but it works both ways. I'm wanting to sing back so badly but I'm too embarrassed to do it by myself. I wish that all of us sitting here sharing this one thing in common, the music, would all forget that we're strangers and just sing back to him in one glorious voice.

The smell of a flower stand in this city
teases my nose with its passing scent
of beauty in its hurried surroundings
like so many quick fleeting thoughts in my head
if grasped might make a worthy poem
or those few daring artists who make me feel less alone
with my crazy thoughts

January 16, 1996
"Ironically, pathology can be a route to soulful religion."
This quote from Thomas Moore's, Care of the Soul, really struck
me because I'm always asking the question, "Why me?" when
bad things happen in my life. This offering that suffering is
really a route to becoming more soulful or deepening your
spirituality is quite comforting. It is really frustrating to think
about the cosmic issue- Why do bad things happen? But this
idea that bad must sometimes happen in order to add depth and
meaning to our lives, makes it much easier to accept evils'
purpose. It is hard to imagine a perfect world where there is no
darkness except that it might become boring. And then again,
maybe my humanity prevents me from imagining such a place. I
guess what I'm getting at is that I feel like a pretty soulful
person. And I've always wondered for what reason have all my
mistakes, misfortunes and just plain sad teen-age years had for
happening? I think Moore's answer would be to give me greater
depth, strength and maybe more understanding? Then why can't
I forgive myself for this part of my life and accept it as a part of
me and my growing experience? Why am I so ashamed of this
past that I can't talk openly about it?
Sometimes I think it will take meeting someone who will tell
me that I'm okay and really mean it. Someone who I can tell
everything to and they will still love me and accept me without
judging. I don't think I'll ever meet this person in this lifetime
though. And ultimately I know what really matters is forgiving
and loving myself.

January 17, 1996

"If we do not claim the soul's power on our own behalf, we become it's victim's. We suffer our emotions rather than feel them working for us." Again I was reading Moore and I have felt both sides of this quote- a victim to my soul's unhappiness and also a great sense of clarity when it is being cared for. Before I started acting, there was little creativity or room for expression in my life. So many of my feelings and desires were repressed, causing them to surface in other destructive ways. Once I was able to freely express what was going on inside myself, I was able to really know my feelings and act more truly to myself. Very little of what I believed, liked or did was because it was a genuine motivation coming from me. I always aimed to please everyone except myself which didn't do anything positive in the long run. It feels so invigorating and also makes me feel independent to be able to really trust my own instincts and form my own philosophies.

"LIVE IN THE MOMENT! DON'T SPEND EVERY SECOND RUNNING FROM IT!" – MAY

At first, it felt like I was running away from my problems. What I now see is that leaving the only life I knew was extremely brave. All I did was truly listen to my instincts, trust myself and stay open to change. Even though at the time I was unable to explain or prove my feelings, I knew I couldn't settle for what direction my life was taking. Deep inside I felt the only way I could ever regain strength and focus to my life was by separating from everything that had caused me self-doubt and hopelessness. I had discovered that I had been searching for happiness in all the wrong places. The materials to make a cocoon within which to heal and emerge anew, had been within myself all along.

I began to feel strong again and realized that I was ready to move into Manhattan on my own. What I wanted more than anything was to pursue acting in the city. My instincts were unmistakable this time; I knew in every fiber of my being that this was the right decision.

YOUNG EYES
I want to play
Please let me out
I hate when you make me
stay inside
So much to see
Trees to climb
Rainbows to follow
Roads to wander
Life to swallow
Young eyes see more
Than age can tell
Don't ever lose your child
or your soul you will sell.

FACING DARKNESS

Before I was able to make yet another new start, I went home to visit my mom and Grandma whose Alzheimer's disease had left her unable to physically care for herself. She hallucinated most of the time and would get so scared that she would lay in bed and cry for hours. Many days she would be convinced that my grandpa who'd been gone now for years, was coming to get her and she'd stand at the front door all day long waiting for him. She'd have her winter coat on and be holding a shopping bag full of her favorite videos and a couple of ashtrays. When we would try to tell her he wasn't coming she'd get angry and swear at us or sometimes she'd just cry. This was only one of hundreds of daily episodes we'd go through with her. Her disease began to sadly fascinate me because of the occasional truths that would jump out of her mouth. She revealed that all of my aunts had different fathers which was never spoken openly about but was suspected. It was as if this disease had manifested itself so that her body and soul could finally cleanse itself of all the secrets and emotions she had hidden for so many years.

I remember you long ago
You seemed so strong and full of life
So many lessons did you teach me
What happened to you?
My child eyes
don't remember you this way
A withering old woman
whose life is only in the past
I find myself wishing
I could release you
into that peaceful place
called death

My mom had written a letter and sent it out to all of our family members about the time I'd left for college asking for help. She and my dad were separated then and she had to care for grandma by herself. Not one single family member responded and we later found out they were angered by the request. True, we had chosen to let my grandparents live with us, but we desperately needed help and were asking for it. Over a few year period, my mom got a few weeks of rest when my grandma went to my aunt's house. I was angry at my family for years after until I finally realized that if I were them, I wouldn't want to deal with the situation either. I actually didn't fully deal with it myself because I was numbed out on drugs and alcohol enough so I didn't have to feel the pain anymore. When grandma almost burnt the house down, we finally decided to put her in nursing home care. This was such a hard decision for my mom because grandpa had the decency of dying in his own home, and she knew grandma wouldn't get the same care or love anywhere else but with her. I guess she just weighed the scales and realized the whole situation had truly broken up the family. Dad was in another state, I was away at school and she wasn't talking to our extended family.

January 18, 1996

I had a really disturbing dream last night that my mom had another child that I didn't know about. I discovered this by reading a letter I had found. In the dream I remember feeling horrified and shocked and even betrayed. It was all so bizarre because in that hazy fog between sleep and awareness, I still believed it was true.

Later I realized that this dream symbolized my own fear of my mother finding out about this other dark side of me. The emotions it stirred, are what I fear my mom will feel when she does find out.

January 28, 1996

I think I'm ready to answer the question asked of me by my tarot reading. "Which are the roles you most easily and often hide behind? Are you ready to drop them?"

The first thing that comes to mind is my role as the "perfect child." This is a role imposed on me by myself which I have been playing my entire life. It is a role of denial and stifles self-awareness. A major fear of mine is that my mother will find out how imperfect her daughter is and blame herself. So it has been very easy most of the time to hide behind a facade of innocence and naivete. Much easier than telling my mother the truth about my teen years. The thought of losing her respect and also knowing she will somehow feel guilty makes me ill. If I knew she would still accept and respect me after knowing this part of my life, it would be the hugest weight off my conscience.

Another role I take on is that of the "peace maker." I'm forever trying to honey coat situations and trying to patch up what's wrong. Between friends, boyfriends, family, etc. I need to just let things be- even if they involve anger, jealousy, shame, hate or frustration. These are very real parts of life whose existence cannot always be hidden.

*

Last issue for me to write about tonight. My fear of having AIDS. I have no real reason to believe that I have it other than knowing I've had unprotected sex. I don't know why I have been putting off getting tested for so long. Ignorance isn't bliss. It is agonizing. There have been many nights I couldn't sleep, worrying about it. And yet this fear still hasn't completely stopped me from doing it. I feel like there is something mentally wrong with me, because once in a while, in the heat of the moment, the condom just doesn't make it's way out of the package. It makes me sick to think about how many times I've prayed to God for one last chance and I swore I'd never have unprotected sex again. I'm not sure if there is an afterlife but I am sure of one thing, we ourselves can create our own living hell on earth.

I was only home for a month, but that was just enough time to get into trouble again. Being home was so unbearable that almost every weekend I went back to school and partied with my friends. I did not know how else to cope with the situation. I felt so ashamed of myself that after all I had changed, I was still too weak to say no to my friends. I felt the depth of my childhood wounds and began to think I was irreparable damaged goods. Needless to say, I was good and ready to go back to New York after the month I had spent at home.

January 28, 1996 *The Power of "X"*
Imagine your body losing all feeling and then being suddenly revived with an overwhelming wave of ecstasy. Your vision is altered and for a moment everything is like a fuzzy TV station. Then you blink and it's as if you are looking at the world through a brand new pair of eyes. Eyes that see only extreme beauty and wonder in everything they meet. People and objects become illumined with a soft white light. All fears, insecurities, and inhibitions are removed. The feeling of love is so overwhelming that just sitting and watching life around you is pleasurable. Sight and sound are so distinctly clear that they seem to be communicating directly with your soul. Music seeps into your pores and is so delicious that it is uncertain which sense is absorbing the sound waves. Touch is so sensitive that everything feels soft and heavenly. It's almost as if you were making love with the universe. You feel like the most self-assured beautiful goddess. The love you feel for your friends and people surrounding you is unlike anything you have ever felt before; you are strangely connected to them in every way.

And then just after you have peaked and are feeling like you've died and gone to heaven, it feels like someone pricked a

60

hole in you and your ecstasy begins to deflate from your body. Life around you turns to normal and people are just ordinary people again. The love and energy oozes out leaving you tired, longing, nervous and alone.

January 29,1996
I feel myself slipping back into old habits, old depression and old lack of self-worth. Thinking about how far I've come in the last few months and what I've achieved depresses me even more. I feel like I've backtracked and everything I have built, my newfound self-acceptance and motivation, is gone. I'm not even all that excited to go back to NY. My determination and hope has been replaced by fear and lack of confidence. I feel like I'm being pulled in half and my body doesn't care which side wins- the side wanting to achieve my dreams or my self-destructive, self-indulgent side. I'm not even feeling sorry for myself- It's more like I'm loathing being me. I feel like an absolutely worthless, dirty piece of trash. All I want to do is sleep where my dreams can create some kind of peace for me.

There's something about nighttime
a cool mystery
Fear melts away
with the setting of the sun
Light can no longer expose
when darkness protects
Erotic thoughts that simmer
below the surface of awareness
Bubble through
into conscious wanting
This shadowy veil of night
Does it protect or tempt me?
When morning comes it seems
that the night is no longer my friend.

61

January 30, 1996

I saw Grandma today at the nursing home. She was so happy to see me and mom. It was strange because the last time I saw her, she barely noticed me. I even asked her if she remembered how to whistle and she looked right at me with a big smile and said, "Sure!" and began to toot. Moments later, her eyes were glossed over and far away again though.

Seeing her made me realize even more how essential it is to embrace life. And yet, I still can't snap out of this depression. I'm really trying to be positive and look forward to the future but I can't force it. I hope this cloud passes over me soon.

Little girl hungers
for something insatiable
Where's her daddy?
Long gone
So who is wrong?
Years spent filling
the hole
Lovers endlessly
unsatisfying
Lost her soul
lost her mind
Where did she get the strength to find
forgiveness?
Finally the lightness came
made her sane
Now she sees beauty
in the rain
Beauty in the darkness
that once consumed her
swallowed her
Made her blind
destroyed her mind

But when will she
find beauty
in the darkness
of the soul
that is her own?

RELEASE

Faced with more new challenges and a burning desire to try again, I was ready to go. With only enough money for my first month's rent and an apartment to move into, I left on a bus for New York City. Even though it seemed a big risk to go there jobless and with very little cash, I had this strange yet comforting feeling that everything would be okay. The farther from home I got, the more my fears began to melt away. Even in the dead of winter the Pennsylvania mountains were a breathtaking sight with their snowcapped tops and leafless trees stretching up towards the endless blue sky. I think solo road trips are good for soul-searching because you are forced to sit and become lost in your own thoughts for long periods of time. While listening to Sarah McLachlan's haunting voice on my headphones, I fantasized about someday being a famous actress and writing a book that helped to make changes in the world.

February 2, 1996

So this is my first night in my new bed. I'm too tired really to know what I'm feeling but I can jot down the evening's events. When I arrived, I went to the wrong address and some man, cute I might add, working on a Whoopi Goldberg film next door, helped me with my bags. Too bad I looked like hell. After 2 days on a bus, my shower felt sooo good. I then went to apply for a job at a restaurant a couple of blocks away where a friend worked. They are going to let me trail Wed. and Thurs. night. Hopefully I've got the job unless I royally mess up. I love my new room. My bed is built up onto a loft and I feel like a little kid trying to boost myself up into it. There is a huge window over-looking a little park area and big glass French doors leading into my room. I am pretty overwhelmed with this new atmosphere. I really can't imagine what my life will be like for the next few months.

February 3, 1996

Tonight in class, May, made a very interesting statement. She explained how it is good to verbalize and actually hear yourself say when you are proud of an accomplishment. By doing this, it makes a feeling more concrete and even more believable. Normally, I would feel egotistical and embarrassed to do that. But it feels like it would be really important for me to get in the habit of doing this more because I too often don't give myself enough credit. I'm my own worst critic and if others are believing in me, then I should have the same respect for myself.

February 4, 1996

I put my walkman on ready to go to bed when an interview with Tori Amos came on. Listening to her soft voice and beautifully soulful responses made me feel a deep respect, admiration and even attraction to her. She said a few things I want to write before I forget. One thing was that there is a "purity in darkness" while talking about her song "Father Lucifer." Just basically allowing certain dark feelings and emotions is healthy. Also she talked about not limiting herself being a woman performer. Music has no race, gender, color-she is absolutely free to feel any kind of song or rhythm. I feel the same way about acting and believe it is such a gift because it is a medium in which all people can touch each other, travelling beyond our human barriers. It is so sad how distanced people are from one another. I feel it in myself everyday. For some reason I never want to get too close physically or emotionally with people. And when I'm alone, I yearn for that closeness.

The first few weeks were very uncertain and trying. Living in the city was very different from the quiet suburb I had lived in during my stay at the acting workshop. A friend helped to get me a job waiting tables which I lost right away supposedly because a former employee wanted her job back. So then I did odd jobs and helped my room mate May with her business for money. At the time, May was producing a play in our studio apartment so I was meeting industry people and getting to see what the business of acting was all about.

A director from a national theater company called May one afternoon to see if she knew any actors that could play a vulnerable girl in high school. Even though I had very little experience she recommended me for the part. When May told me about the audition and gave me the character description I could not believe my ears. The night before I had written a monologue for myself about a girl in high school! This was an exciting coincidence!!

February 15, 1996: Audition Monologue

"I'm sorry but I can't be with you anymore. Don't worry it's not another guy. I'm restless. There was a time when our relationship was so fulfilling, but that's gone now. I know this will sound strange but I've had this kind of spiritual revelation. I realized that because I was with you I had given away a part of myself before I was even whole. What I mean is that I don't really know who I am by myself without you. So much of what I think and do and say is what you would think or do or say. You're not understanding this are you? Ok. Let me be a little more clear. Last week, when I told you I was staying after school with my biology teacher... I lied. I tried out for the school play. I got this urge to take a risk, try something different. And ya know what? It was the most amazing experience! When I was on that stage the rest of the world disappeared.

So what does this have to do with you?? This has everything to do with you! I had an experience that changed me and there's no way of turning back. It made life different somehow. The wholeness I used to feel with you I felt by myself on that stage. It was exhilarating, and intense and inspiring and I was alone! And now when I'm with you life seems ordinary again. I know

*I'm hurting you and I hate myself for that. But I know in my soul
I can't forget what happened to me on that stage."*

May coached me privately over the next week and I
practiced every chance I could. I made it through all of the
callbacks and booked the understudy role of Mandy in a national
tour called "Halfway There." My first New York audition and I
had booked something! I was told the chances of that were a
million in one. The play toured around the country to schools
doing a wonderful show about teens who had lost their way and
ended up in rehab to rediscover themselves. Learning my lines
and working on the character Mandy was easy because I
practically was her. Being part of this show finally enabled me
to confront and express much of the pain I had buried inside
myself. I was able to release many of the dark emotions that had
hidden within me and had manifested themselves through my
destructive behavior for so long. Only now I had a healthy way
to express them.

"Look at me. I'm just the little girl your crayons painted
blue. I don't want to be a child anymore. But I'm afraid, that if
I let go, all the fantasy and illusion will fade. So it isn't easy
being in the middle. One minute in the sandbox... and the next
falling in love."

"Halfway There" by Sunna Rash

February 28, 1996
*I am so excited!! I just got a phone call that I got the
understudy role! I'm actually relieved at this because I'm able
to experience being a part of this theatre company, being paid,
but not the immediate pressure of performing. I am so proud of
myself and this just reinforces that I made the right decision to
be here.*

68

I didn't realize until today how truly important this show is to me. Not just the money or experience but actually being a part of this show. I mean, to be able to reach kids, maybe preventing them from what I went through or just to let them know that they aren't alone. If I had something like this when I was having all of my teen problems, maybe I could have been stronger and not have lost so much of myself. I had a flashback of wanting to talk about rape to high school kids someday and this is kind of my chance.

There is a storm in my soul
thunder rumbles
in the pit of silence
Lightning legs streak
across the darkest skies
Only shadowy echoes
and silhouettes are discerned
in this strangely dim light
I'm stilled by my fear
yet drawn into the mystery
of this electrical sea
in my heart
Divided in two
touching only at that fine line
attached
yet always apart

This was just one of many experiences that showed me how truly healing it was to uncover and deal with painful feelings. I felt how harmful it was to deny these dark experiences and saw the repercussions in my own life. For years, I ran away from my pain instead of facing it and dealing with it. Our fear of judgment by others or worst of all ourselves, keeps us from exploring or even admitting to the so-called mistakes we have made. So we stuff our stuff and pretend it never happened but the truth is, it never goes away.

February 16,1996

After another amazing class, Faith and I took a walk in Central Park and had a great conversation. I can tell that she is going to succeed in this business. There is something experienced and yet innocent about her. She is really okay with herself and with being different. She talked about how moving to NY and living here for 10 years has made her feel kind of "insulated." I hope to get to know her better because she makes me feel very comfortable with just being myself.

I need to just let people see my vulnerability and naivete and stop trying to appear so strong and together all the time when I'm not. I'm really starting to believe in my potential and gift of awareness as a living breathing thing. I need to just take the risk of allowing myself to just be.

This has most definitely been an evening of reaching some deeper levels of awareness. I feel so cleansed and grounded and exhausted all over my entire body and being. I feel so grateful for life, no for My life at this moment.

February 18, 1996

I feel so exposed and uncomfortable and sick to my stomach right now. I told May a little bit about my sexual past, more than I've ever told one person at any one time. She says that she doesn't feel that I'm a bad person but that I feel that way and I slowly need to heal the part of myself living in the past. I'm just starting to see that my sexuality affects so much of my life and that I really have to start dealing with this part of myself

February 19, 1996

This morning I woke up exactly how I went to bed and that really scares me. My chest is heavy, literally, from carrying so

70

much pain in my heart. I threw out my cigarettes, I never should have started again, and I'm not drinking again until I feel really good. I want to start off the day by exercising and get into a routine again and I'm going to eat healthy. I'm really scared about how I feel. I feel old and worn out and used up. I'm beginning to feel like I'll never be an actress and if that's so then I don't know why I'm alive or what my purpose is.

*

Well, thank God those feelings have left me. It amazes me that I even wrote those words just this morning. I did some really great work on my monologue today and even performed in front of May's cast members. I'm really proud of myself. I feel so emotionally raw right now that life seems kind of like a dreamy haze and I can't get grounded.

I know I took a huge risk last night by telling May about my problem with my sexuality and the fear I have of AIDS. I still feel uncomfortable with having exposed that, but it is something I think I'll be more able to deal with soon.

Something I really love about May is that she is one of the only adults I know who thinks it is important to have dreams and really believe that you can reach them. She helped me to believe that it is more than possible for me to get onto a soap or even a movie someday. Just the thought that that could happen is amazing to me. I want all the people who ever doubted me or made me feel small to see that I am capable of anything. I want my father to see me on TV and know that that is the little girl he never knew. But more importantly I want this to happen because I deserve it and because I'll work hard to make it happen.

For some reason, anything seems possible at night. Like Sara sings, " it's morning that I dread, another day of knowing, the path I fear to tread."

In my own experience, what I discovered is that we are born into this world innocent and pure. Throughout life, in order to cope with our pains and disappointment we build walls to avoid feeling the hurt. These walls can be anything from a tough attitude to harsh sarcasm to indifference. Tidy little barriers that act like gates to our hearts. Do you remember the first time someone hurt you, how painful that was ?? It seems normal that our tendency would be to protect ourselves. But after many years of building these walls, I believe it becomes difficult to reach within ourselves and touch that innocence, that true inner person. Not being in contact with that inner self, we lose touch with what truly fulfills us, what makes us happy. We then begin to look outside of ourselves for fulfillment. We look to our lovers, our children, our jobs, our friends, everyone but ourselves to fulfill us. Computers, cars, movies and shopping become our only way to have fun and find a sense of happiness. And many times when these essential people and things disappoint us, we turn to the escape of alcohol, drugs, sex, gangs, violence and other destructive acts. Being unable to find fulfillment in a healthy way, we search for ways to express and satisfy ourselves. Less obvious manifestations of being unfulfilled, but just as harmful to people's lives are greed for money or power, eating disorders, lack of self-worth and hundreds of others. Each seeming failure to find this happiness leads to discontentment and we begin to grow cynical feeling like victims to life. The optimism and innocence of youth slowly fades while we become harder, more separate from our fellow human beings and less likely to try and change things.

March 2, 1996
Class was very productive today. Everyone had to share what they were scared of and I was able to voice, for the first time, my fear of AIDS. Also how my problems with sexuality affects my relationships. I felt a connection to everyone in the group today and felt like I could trust them all. I see us growing as a class

together. I am ready to go to the gyne and get tested for HIV, so this is the week. Whatever the outcome, I can't live life anymore without knowing.

March 5, 1996
I get so scared sometimes that I've damaged parts of my mind that will never recover and that I may never reach the full potential that I could have. After watching "Scent of a Woman" tonight, I felt a strange mixture of sadness, respect and joy. Watching an amazing actor like Pacino makes me feel like I'll never even come close to reaching the depths he does. Until I began acting, I always thought it looked so easy. Now I know it is one of the most challenging, emotionally risk taking and brave professions known. Actors have made it their business to explore the spectrum of human emotion and feel what most of us avoid feeling. It makes me either want to give up acting all together or completely devote my life to it.

March 12, 1996
I think a big problem with people is that we try to see ourselves through other people. What I mean is that we look to others to give us feedback about ourselves and may sometimes even look to get acceptance of ourselves. The problem is though, that people may not always give honest responses to you. They may act like they hate your guts but are really madly in love with you. They may consciously not even know what they feel about you. So that's where the games begin. Trying to figure out the subtext of people.
So how can you truly ever "see" yourself? I believe that the answers can all come from within you. If you really listen to yourself, your instincts and trust your judgement then you can just Know yourself.

A wise book, the Healing Runes, once counseled me, "...look within and take stock, make a fearless personal and moral inventory of your life...open yourself up and let the Light into a part of your life that has been secret, shut away...the time has finally come to end the dance of Denial... When something within us is disowned, that which is disowned wreaks havoc." Until I took the time to look at my past and heal it, the layers of old memories and emotion weighed on my soul and conscience like a steel anchor. Until I learned how to express and release the past, it prevented me from ever truly moving forward and succeeding in life. Although it was scary to look my darkness in the face, when I looked at it, I realized why it was there. It wasn't because I was a "bad" person, or any of the other names I'd been called throughout my life. It was because, I had let life steer me away from my own heart and who I Really was.

Every time I worked on my character, whether in my acting class or at play practice, I felt the old layers coming away. I was like a mummy being slowly unwrapped from suffocating layers of pain. My healing journey had begun.

A HEALING JOURNEY

Just as I was really getting worried about my financial situation, another coincidence occurred when a girl I had met through the play asked if I knew anyone in need of a job. Because I was an understudy I didn't get to go on tour and so I started temping for her the following week. For three months I worked 9 to 5 in an office. The most difficult part about the job was witnessing how unhappy most of the wonderful people I worked with were. I was an unbiased outsider looking in on all of the dramas they created and the roles they methodically played. Ironically, some of my most creative writing took place in the midst of all the commotion around me, including the start of this book. I think writing helped me to escape from the office when it became too intense.

Looking out my window at the dirty street below I wonder what their lives are like watching the faceless people go by like ghosts off to their 9 to 5 home to his pretty wife do you know life better than I?

HEURISTIC BIAS
Ms. Corporate Big Thing
How's your life today?
Can you see past that stack of papers in your way?
Told the man on the phone
you were in a big meeting
I didn't realize that meant
getting your nails done and eating
So your name starts with Ms.
Well that says it all
I wonder if love ever climbed your walls
Your appetite for power
has left you on top of it all
But be prepared for a much harder fall

than the colored boy you screamed at
for bringing your coffee late
I feel sad for you
One day you'll wake up and say
What for??

I'd like to comment on this poem and why it's entitled Heuristic Bias. A heuristic bias is predetermining without all the facts. I wrote this about a powerful woman I worked for who is the director of an international company. I was very intimidated by this woman and wrote the poem in anger and judgement of her. One day, I nervously asked if I could interview her for a powerful character I was working on in acting class. More personally though, I wanted to see behind her "walls" and prove for myself that there was a good person inside of her tough exterior. It turned out that love had "climbed her walls," and he'd died when she was a teen. He was her one and only true love. She was of Spanish descent, and always felt she had to prove herself, being ethnic and a woman. She worked very hard to achieve her goals and became the director of this prominent corporation, her toughness and conviction seeming to be what got her there. But that day, she let me see a softer side, a woman who would die to save the life of an animal or child. A woman who has risen to many challenges and overcome them. I think that I was so intimidated by her because I've met few powerful women in my life. I hope if she reads this today, she will hear me when I tell her how beautiful that other side was. I hope she finds joy and softness in he life. And I want to thank her for teaching me never, to judge anyone, without first getting all the facts.

A few months later, money was still tight so I took another job at a restaurant involving the fashion industry. It was fun for a while because it gave me a chance to check in with mainstream again. After a few weeks there, I remembered why I so often checked out of society and its trendiness. Pretty painted faces with starving bodies running to the restroom after their meal. Working there made me feel insecure again, like I had to lose fifteen pounds and go shopping for new clothes. As much as I needed the money I could not stand working there anymore. So I quit.

So you have the latest fashion
and you've got the whitest smile
Your boyfriend is Mr. Perfect
Are you happy for a while?
Afraid to look beyond the mirror
for what may lie inside
Remember your illusions
are impossible to hide.

Which now brings me to the subject of how destructive the whole glamour scene in fashion and TV is on young girls and women's self -esteem. I don't need to quote statistics for this to be displayed as a problem. Everywhere I go I see teens and adults so skinny they could be mistaken for pre-pubescent. Many of my friends have been anorexic, bulimic and I also have suffered from anemia. One afternoon while shopping with one of my best friends, she complained for the seventeenth million time that day, about being fat- she's 5'6", maybe 105 lbs., and could easily be a J. Crew model. Irritated, I very curtly retorted, "Will you stop, you look like a 14 year old." Underneath my anger was frustration at not knowing how to help her when she very obviously has a problem. And it is understandable, when every time we look at a fashion magazine or turn on the TV, we're bombarded with images of beautiful, thin, picture perfect people. Even after all of the work I've done on my self image, when I'm exposed to this, I begin to feel insecure and not beautiful enough. I think beauty needs to be redefined in the world and left not only to the thin and glamorous. Magazines and television need to start portraying a more "real" image of people and the world.

But we also need to start requesting that to happen. Counselors trained in this area should be available in schools for young people to talk to. Girls need to be encouraged to discover and strive for more than just physical beauty. Their talents, kindness, and intelligence are incredibly beautiful as well.

During the time I was in New York I had been taking acting classes with my roommate May, I'd met through the workshop. I called it my acting/therapy. The technique I was studying deals with the body as an instrument that always has to be fine- tuned. This is accomplished by removing any emotional residue that has built up inside. If an actor was preoccupied with his/her own frustrations, anger, insecurities, it was harder to create a clean character from a messy emotional state. So we had many exercises that helped to release all of this old stored up emotion. Which also worked in my real life too- I was able to much more creatively and clearly deal with my life issues. Not carrying so much "emotional baggage," I had more energy to give to all areas of my life. Each class, little by little, I would let go and express different experiences or emotions I had been holding on to or hiding. Layer after layer would peel off my soul leaving me closer to that forgotten person inside. After each class I would feel lighter, as if rocks were removed from my body or cleansed like after a good hard cry.

For a while, I thought class was magical and that it was the only place where amazing things happened in my life. I watched people, including myself, heal from traumatic life experiences. I saw that I was not the only one who had deep insecurities and regrets. I experienced a kind of chain reaction- as one person exposed their issues, it gave others the courage to do the same. People were able to completely express themselves and deal with these issues they did not feel safe exposing outside of class. I was able to talk about my rape, drug and alcohol abuse and my deep fear of AIDS which no longer felt so overwhelming after expressing it. For the first time, I saw men showing real emotion, allowing themselves to cry and let down the tough exterior they'd been taught to believe was essential. My heart would open and expand in gratitude for being honored to see people be so real, so vulnerable. I saw glimpses of my classmates "inner selves" and they were so beautiful and kind and loving. I saw a common theme that all we were really looking for in our lives was love and acceptance. And we judged ourselves so harshly, hid, and put up walls around anything we thought would stand in the way of acquiring that love. In the classroom, I experienced a way of relating with people that felt so right and much more in alignment with who we are at the core. I felt that if major amounts of people could experience what I did, it could change the world. If children grew up with this kind of openness, expression and emotional honesty, by the time they reached adulthood, they wouldn't be so layered.

After three hours of feeling alive, nurtured, accepted and cleansed, I would return to the "real world." Sounds of reality would echo in my ears as sirens screamed by, off to put out another fire or rush another victim to the hospital. It became too painful to remain open and vulnerable in this chaotic world. People seemed irritated by my joy or skeptical of it and my openness made them uncomfortable. My optimism waned and the protective shields would return. An overwhelming feeling of longing and restlessness would loom over me until my next class. I wanted so badly to feel that same magic in my life every day. And that is when the realization dawned that it was completely possible to live life how I have been longing to for years. Class did not have to be the only place I felt so fully alive.

April 18, 1996

I feel as if I've been reborn into life again. When I think about how far I've come in the last six months it amazes me. I still have these contradicting emotions though. Some days I feel like anything is possible and others it feels like life is purely survival. But life Feels different now. I see things that maybe I noticed as a child but as I grew up became too distracted by my everyday dramas to notice. Like now, I'm sitting on the ground looking up at the towering buildings against the midnight blue sky. There is an American flag that caught my eye. What fascinates me is the way the reflection of the flag looks in the window of the building it is hanging from. The colors are still their prominent red, white and blue but in the reflection there is this luminescent sheen making the image appear beautifully surreal. My mind starts playing and I'm thinking about how this image relates to people. This image symbolizes how so many humans see themselves and life. Like the flag, we just accept what we so often see. But through the reflection of something or someone else, we are able to catch that faint shimmer of light we can't always see in ourselves. Like when someone gives you a great compliment or a teacher praises your work or if someone is attracted to you. That uniqueness that others may see in you, may only be seen by you through others. It's difficult to look into ourselves for acceptance so we begin to look to other people for it. And unfortunately, many people will never be truthful in their feelings about you. Not everyone is willing to compliment or validate us. So then we begin to doubt ourselves and our judgment because we're always looking to each other for approval. I guess the secret is in learning to love, trust and know ourselves.

*

What a gift it is to be able to use your uniqueness and reveal your soul to affect others. A good actor can affect even the most

81

hardened people. I've witnessed a few beautiful moments such as these with my stepfather who is pretty guarded emotionally. Growing up, we weren't really close in a traditional sense, but have always had this sort of unspoken love and respect for each other. Some of the few great moments of love that I have felt for him have been while watching a powerfully sad movie together, usually a love story. (He's a romantic at heart although he'd never admit it.) I'd look at him out of the corner of my eye and see one big tear running down his cheek that he didn't dare wipe away because then it would be like crying aloud. Seeing this would tear me apart and I'd feel the pain and frustration and loss of his entire life in that one tiny tear.

My experiences with the acting workshop, drama classes, working on my understudy role and hundreds of hours of journaling, confirmed for me that healing just about anything is possible, and with that healing comes great joy and inspiration. When I finally moved through the old layers, I began to discover who I really was and what I wanted out of life. As I looked at, owned and learned everything about me, I could then begin to love and trust myself. Once I began trusting my instincts and faced my fear of change, the real changes in my life began to occur. I stayed open to the opportunities in my life and began to see new doorways opening both without and within. Every experience became a stepping stone leading me closer to my true self and my destiny. It was as if, once I made up my mind to find out who I truly was, the universe began working for me instead of against me. With a bit of time, lots of determination and a desire to really know yourself, you can do it too.

Now think back
to a time long past
When you were an innocent child
unbiased to the ways of the world
What hurt that closed you off?

Was it your cold mother
or a father who drank?
Were you teased because
of your unusual face?
Was learning hard and they branded you dumb?
Was your family poor
so you worked
while the other children played
and had fun?
Maybe you were the middle child
and never could compare
to the eldest or the baby
it just wasn't fair
So you learned how to Not feel the hurt
You protected yourself
Oh the layers you built
Adulthood approached
and some of you grew insecure
while others became driven
But do you see these obstacles were given
to help you grow strong
and wise to the world
Not afraid and withdrawn
disillusioned and cynical
It's never too late
to look at the past
Make peace with these feelings
that seem everlasting
Forgive yourself
and the ones who caused this pain
Unleash the darkness that festered such hate
The more people who break
through their walls of fear
the less separate we'll be
By releasing yourself you set others free

from the regrets and the sadness
you have possessed for so long
We're all here to learn
make mistakes
and many times be wrong
Forget your ego
and your useless pride
Don't be a prisoner to society
Step to the other side
Beyond your limiting boundaries
Open your mind
and allow yourself to believe
that this world can change
We hold the power
to end the misery.

HOPE RESTORED

April 20, 1996

I was drawn to Central Park today. It's a perfect spring day, the air is cool with a hint of warmth, the sun is shining through the ever-shifting clouds. I've decided this is my new favorite place to escape. Today I'm just letting nature heal me by laying on the huge rock formations or sitting up against trees. If it weren't for all of the skyscrapers staring down on me through the treetops, I could forget I'm in NY. I've found a spot high up on one of the huge rocks that my body fits into perfectly when I lay on my back. It slopes slightly forward so that I can see the entire playground while lying down. The city sounds are pleasantly muffled and far away but the occasional screaming child keeps me from falling asleep. I feel exhausted and invigorated all at once. I enjoy people watching and there is a couple that I'm strangely drawn to. She has golden hair falling down to the top of her perfectly shaped hips. He's laying on his back, arms behind his head, smiling up at her while she playfully hangs on the fence. I wonder what they are thinking about. I wonder what people think when they see me barefoot in my work clothes perched on this rock observing and scribbling in my notebook My butt is starting to get sore and I remember a time when my body never ached from stress and working. I'm feeling painfully happy right now, like I could cry tears of joy or burst into laughter at any moment. And I wonder why is life so beautifully sad and sadly beautiful? Some day, when I'm feeling courageous enough, I want to put on my green cord overalls and come here again and play. Just be a child again for one day. I want to climb these rocks and pretend I'm on some strange Star Trek planet. I'll play until I'm totally exhausted or until I scrape my hands and knees and have to go home. But for now, my lunch break is over and I have to get back to work.

October 18, 1996

Two nights ago Tom Selleck came into the restaurant while I was working. I couldn't believe that one of my favorite childhood stars who I'd grown up on, was sitting less than fifteen feet from my cash register. I went through all kinds of mixed emotions ranging from excitement to depression because he represents the dream that seems so far away. The last half hour he was there, I kept getting this overwhelming need to write a poem about him. I can't even remember what I wrote him now although I know it wasn't sleazy. So I ended up giving it to the doorman who then gave it to him. After the fact, I fantasized that he sent me flowers the next day and then put the thought out of my head because it was becoming painfully embarrassing to think about what I'd done. The funny thing was that it didn't stay out of my head long because when I got home my roommate was watching an old Magnum episode. When I told Mark what I did, he just looked at me in disbelief like he half admired me and half thought I was nuts.

So yesterday I rushed around like an idiot trying to get my errands done, get to my two hour hair appointment and get to work on time. I spent about 20 of those minutes in the bathroom crying because the stylist butchered my already short hair. I managed to get to work just in time to do my routine before the pre-theatre rush started. So I didn't pay much attention when the phone rang but when the maitre'd said dramatically, "Yes, Meggan McAndrews (my birth name) is here," I thought, could it be... and he handed me the phone. The second I heard the voice on the other end I just about went into shock. He said to me, "Hi Meggan, this is Tom Selleck." I grabbed onto the marble bar to contain myself. I don't remember much of the conversation other than sounding exactly how I did not want to the first time I talked to a star. I melted when he told me the poem had touched him and he wanted to say thank you and ask why I hadn't delivered it myself?! Ugh!! He then asked me what days I worked and said he'd try to come in and thank me personally!

Well, some wonderful things certainly came out of this experience. I had been having trouble with a character in acting class who was supposed to act "elated" in one scene. I couldn't make her elated because I had never felt it before in my own life. And elation would pretty much describe what I felt after that phone call. What else has really struck me, is the importance of following my instincts even when they seem crazy. This was good enough proof that taking risks can have undreamed of results. Most importantly though, that my writing touched him enough for Tom Selleck to take time out of his busy schedule to thank me. Even if I never meet the man, this has already been a grand experience.

The magic returned to my life when I finally realized that at the core of a human being, lies more power than most of us will ever allow ourselves to see. Each of us hold all the answers we need to survive, grow and to claim our own destiny. Like the turtle who hides within its shell or the flowers that bud in the spring, we have the instincts to protect ourselves and survive. And underneath our layers lies an even greater power- our never ending ability to love. Once I was able to truly love and accept myself I became more compassionate towards humanity and all of our struggles. The fulfillment I had been searching for my entire life outside of myself was really all about finding love and peace within. That is why I am writing this book. I love this world and I believe that you can love and discover yourself until this connection has finally united every person across the planet.

I know this vision seems a little large, but it doesn't even come close to the greatness that is inside each and every one of us. If you let yourself believe in this possibility, that you have a unique purpose for being here, your life Will change. Everything you do, in every moment matters- your very being alive matters.

April 24, 1996

I've started reading another book that within the first few pages has already taken me to another level. What amazes me the most, is how so much of what I'm learning from all these books, I have always known on some level within myself. The words just seem to solidify the feelings and help give clarity to my understanding.

Something else I've been feeling is my own power. It scares me because I know how I affect people. I can easily bring happiness to someone and then crush them the next. I see how just one person's negativity ripples out and affects others. With this awareness comes a new responsibility in how to interact with and treat people. I wish with all my heart I could go back and change how I've treated certain people, especially past relationships.

*

Some of my co-workers were having a conversation about religion today and it's an issue that I think I'm finally ready to have an opinion on. From the little that I know about organized religion it promotes too much conformity and not enough self-expression and self-cultivation. And yet religion seems to give many people a base or core that I think is essential or we'd have no morals. If only religion could be like a mother- nurture and provide for a human soul while it is still young and impressionable, and then one day let it go to its own lessons and find its way back to itself where the true learning and growing begins.

*

A memory surfaced today from childhood that confirmed something I've always known. Since I was little, I have known that I was unique and I understood things about life before I even knew the words to express this. I used to become overwhelmed with an unexplainable sadness and cry and cry until my mom would calm me. I think my child eyes saw things raw, at their very core and would many times become overwhelmed. I felt the shadow of sadness cast over life the first time I heard "Puff the Magic Dragon." Something in that song revealed to me, all the beauty and emptiness in the world.

*

May and I just had a beautiful conversation. The more I see the person she is, the more I am able to be the person I am. Finally, I've met a person who doesn't get caught up in all the little details of life, but looks for the bigger meanings and truths.

April 25, 1996
I find it ironic that most of my learning and growing spiritually has taken place in an office behind a reception desk. In between answering phones and mindless small talk, I have been able to read books that are changing my life. I am really starting to See, as if for the first time. Things that made no sense or were overwhelming in my past are now coming to me with much more clarity. Some ideas are still fuzzy and I haven't quite grasped them, but I know they will come in time. There is no real sense of urgency to do anything except keep reading and reflecting on everything I can. It is so strange how time has no real meaning for me anymore except in terms of being to a job or appointment on time.

October 10, 1996
So here's the start of yet another new journal. I began writing pretty regularly about a year ago when I moved to New York. It was a way for me to express all of the swirling thoughts in my head and gain some clarity. My notebook became my best friend because it never failed to be there for me whether it was

the middle of the night or I was too emotional to talk. It became this unbiased, non-judgmental confessional, having absolutely no care about what I was writing, a place of complete freedom. And yet its empty pages seemed to encourage me to fill them and give them color. What more could I ask for from a friend?

And now when I go back and read entries from over the past year, I'm filled with all kinds of mixed feelings and memories. Part of me feels embarrassed by things I've said and done while another part finds pleasure in seeing my own progression. I'm also proud of the book that emerged out of the self-discovery due to regularly journaling. There is delicious satisfaction in having learned how to tap into this talent and discovering that I do have unique gifts.

Even though there is uncertainty about the future, there is a difference in the way I perceive and approach it. First off, I actually care about my future which for a long time I didn't. There is also an excitement and mystery about its unfolding. Every day dramas are not as all-encompassing anymore. I have found a profound peace in some of the knowledge that I've gained about the world and my own purpose in it. I've realized that the only battle that really matters in the end, is the one with self.

FACELESS VISION
Emerald eyes
peer into the darkness
Delicate fingers
part the spider webs
entangled in their
soft stickiness
Only haunting shadows
linger before this young maiden
Lusting for a treasure
only she can claim
Holding no map

90

to show her the way
Slowly
bare feet move across
the dusty cold floor
Longing to feel damp grass
beneath them again
She lights a torch in hopes
it will melt the blackness before her
The emptiness of time swells in
like a giant looming regret
whispering in the sleeping mind
She speaks to herself,
"Fear not, it is your heart that leads
into the unknown
I do not know what awaits me,
on the other side
yet I feel it will be
what words cannot justly color"
And on she continues
with the dream of a faceless vision
drawing her submissively
into its arms

TIME FOR CHANGE

I do not want to mislead you into thinking that change happens easily or even quickly. Removing a lifetime of negative habits and layers is a challenging process. As humans we are programmed how to think and be from the time we enter this world. Unlearning things you have been taught and grown comfortable with is a scary thing. Many people are afraid to even question their beliefs let alone change them. So you are very brave for even having the desire to undergo self-examination and being open to change.

When we are born, we are innocent and helpless. We are dependent on our family members or caretakers to survive. As we grow older, we learn that certain behavior is approved of by them or disapproved of. And that "good" behavior results in feelings of comfort and approval whereas "bad" behavior results in discomfort or even pain. We accept this because these people are the only source for love and guidance that we know. Even when these beliefs are dysfunctional we take them on because we know nothing different. All families hold different beliefs and standards, so no one child is really taught the same "rules." Problems arise often because the world is filled with people who have different beliefs and so called "morals."

As the years pass, we learn that fitting in feels good and we rarely question what we do or say to fit in. We look to the people around us and the world in general for acceptance and do whatever we know to get approval. When I did things that I knew the people I looked up to would not approve of, I felt the need to hide them. That is when the walls start being built, either from our own feelings of wrong-doing or to shield against the pain someone has caused us. Someone with unloving parents might take on a cold, aggressive nature, while someone with overbearing parents might become shy. A child may have parents that expect too much and they become over-achievers, hiding themselves behind their talents. Or in the extreme cases, a child who was abused, may become so detached from feeling, that he becomes a serial killer.

I was too young to realize that my family and society had programmed me with certain beliefs and ways of being. Some beliefs I held were, that men are stronger than women, women are here to serve men, sex should be kept hush hush, and many others. I had accepted their views of life and did whatever I had to fit in. Even if it meant lying to myself and to them. The person who I am now doesn't believe these things, but they were so engrained in my being, that when I couldn't live up to these standards I felt like a failure. Because I felt so low, it was easy for me to escape into drugs, sex and alcohol. I didn't know who I was anyways. I never had a chance to create who I was- my family and society did that for me. Which is why I am unraveling myself now, to find out who I Really Am.

On my journey towards better self-awareness. I fell back into old traps many times and am still often tempted by my old lifestyle of escapes. There is a part of me that kicks and fights awareness and wants to forever remain an irresponsible child. But the lessons I have learned from my mistakes have been good medicine. There is a certain sadness about looking reality in the face and accepting there are no easy rides in life. Even the rich and famous are human and undergo struggles like we do. A moment comes where you accept responsibility for your life or you forever blame it on outside events and people. We may not always feel like we have choices in life, but we do. We can always choose to turn even the most painful experiences into positive ones. Pain can be a powerful motivator and push us harder to fulfill our dreams. Again, this book is an example of just that. I could have continued to feel sorry for myself and continued on a downward spiral. Instead I opted for change, and used my life experiences to help me grow and am able to happily share this with you today.

What has reassured me and will help you is when you begin to see and feel how much more fulfilling life becomes without old negative tendencies. This is because when you discover your own dreams, you will be living your own life and the happiness it brings you will spread to others.

Sometimes you may be so filled with joy and try to reach out to someone who just isn't ready to be reached. There are some people who have held beliefs for so long they don't know how to let them go. Some people may even try and prevent your growth because ultimately it means they will have to face their fear of change and grow too. But I know you will find the strength within you to continue to learn and grow and spread your joy to those who are willing to accept it. I read an amazing book that found its way to me that explains how I feel about being closed-minded better than I could express. Ramtha said, "You know, the atrocity of being closed-minded is that it keeps you from knowing joy. It keeps you enslaved to the illusions of man. It keeps you from knowing the glory of yourself... As long as you have a cloistered mind and live and think according to social consciousness, you will never venture into the unknown or contemplate the possibility of greater realities for fear that it will mean change... As long as you accept only those limited thoughts that are bred into you, you will never activate greater portions of your brain to receive and experience any thought other than what you have faced every day of your existence."

Prisoners to our minds
locked behind doors
of limited thinking
Yet freedom lies
just beyond our grasp
Keep reaching in
for the desire to know
And soon we will fly to heights
beyond this despairing illusion.

July 25, 1996

I just watched the movie "Kids" and I feel greatly disturbed. What is scary to me is that I did not grow up in NYC where the filming took place, I grew up in the middle class suburbs of midwestern America and yet I was still able to relate to everything that was happening. This sickness of hopelessness in our youth is not just in the inner cities, its deathly web stretches out across the entire country and over oceans across the planet. It sickens me that this world is so overwhelming to kids that they fall into the abysmal escape that drugs provide. We are the product of our parents mistakes and their parents mistakes and so on and so on and we have to climb out of their cesspool just to stay alive. And if we live... some of us feel, what for? To spend our lives trying to fix their mistakes while trying not to make our own?

At one time, I was Jenny. Innocent girl who lost her self esteem and did drugs because... why not? Someone put them in my face and that was the only thing besides sex that made me feel good. Or rather, not feel anything at all. I could not see beyond what was happening in the moment because life just seemed too fucking overwhelming. And the times I really tried to think about the future, what was there to look forward to? The options I saw were my parents life and they could never seem to find happiness or my grandparents who both died of horrible diseases after living horrible lives or maybe I could work 9 to 5 and try to find happiness through my kids. Nothing appealed to me so I lived in the moment and tried not to think about the future. Ironically, that became my survival.

This sounds a little different from the girl who believes in world peace. Well, it takes more than optimism and dreaming. I live in the reality of NYC now where I see the best and worst of everything. Every day I am affected by what is happening around me. Even when I try and hide in my apartment away

96

from the world, it infiltrates in by way of my TV or the newspaper or the sounds of sirens coming through my closed windows. There are times I want to scream out my window, "World, this is a wake up call! You are not alone in your feelings of despair! But we are not beyond changing things! I'm trying to make a difference here but I need help!" And that's how I feel. It is going to take many individuals reaching within themselves and discovering in what small way they can make a difference

GENERATION LOST
We are the lost generation
Nothing to look forward to
so we live in the moment
We live for escape
Expressing who we think
we are
Our minds like zombies
We pierce
tatoo
abuse our bodies
We pray to the Drug God
He is the savior of our pain
Sex is our offering
We're submissive
enslaved
Night an addiction
pulsing in our veins
Our eyes only see
in the dark
We drink music for substance
Morning sets us apart
from your society
Look at what you've created
An underground world

that feels forgotten
and hated.

Recently a friend of mine who lived through the 1960's brought an important point to my attention. She feels that her generation is not given the full credit deserved and is often just referred to as a time of drugs and "free love." The people of the 60's truly prepared future generations with so much we often take for granted. They were true soul-searchers who demanded an awareness of issues such as drug abuse and alcoholism, child and sexual abuse, racial and gender discrimination, gay right's, environmental concerns and many other issues ignored by society. Their pains motivated them to dedicate their lives to changing things. It may seem to many like the 60's were an explosion of recklessness but to me, they epitomize what can happen when our self-expression is dammed up within. Sooner or later it is going to come busting through in unproductive ways.

Nowadays, all we have to do is look in the yellow pages for what support group suits our need. The younger generations have all the power and information we need to help in the healing process of this planet. But first we must begin to heal ourselves.

In a major magazine, they began an article about teens with these words, "If you went by the headlines, here is what you'd believe: that teens are promiscuous, sniffing, snorting, shooting, unduly pierced, gun-toting demons who are a danger to themselves and those around them... They have unprotected sex, conceive children, then leave them in garbage bins...They all probably should have been put on Ritalin from the time they started teething... Is this a fair picture of the 27 million 13 to 19 year olds?" I certainly don't think so. I believe the youth of America has the ability to prove those who believe this Wrong. We can use the positive gifts our ancestors have left us and even undo some of the messes they have made. If we can start

98

cleaning up our own acts and stop feeling so helpless, I know we can make great changes in the world. After all, we are tomorrow's leaders so lets do it right and with some style!

Trance me enhance me do that groovy dance me
dissolve me solve me find me my analogy
provoke me smoke me bruise and beat and choke me
cheese me sleaze me can't you see she's fluffy?
truce me let me unloose me love the universe me
phish me I wish me could swim in your psychedelic sea
echo me agree with me please find your own mind me
intrigue me give me ecstasy then leave me
CHAOS ME BLIND ME ROB ME OF MY SOUL ME
unity could it be a way of living life me?
pollute me dilute the seas with your wasted energy
religion me talk at me and through me the blind can't see
love me daddy your forgotten baby will you ever know me?
shoot me gang me leave me homeless on the streets
elect me select me I'll waste your money and ignore world tragedy
snort me import me take me intravenously I'll put your mind at ease
crucify me slaughter me you find this is your serenity
CHAOS ME BLIND ME ROB ME OF MY SOUL ME
beauty me skinny me make me look like those people on tv
educate me don't drown me in your life philosophy
rape me take me down and make me hate me
cage me I'm a monkey here to free you of disease
sell me I am cheap let me make you money from the streets
ignore me poor me I'm just your conscience don't worry
heaven me hell me it's a long ways away from me
soul me find me it's the only way to world peace.

Over the last few years I have traveled a lot and have met kids from all over the country. I've observed a common theme

99

of hopelessness or of extreme ignorance to the world around them. All that is important to many young adults is what is happening right in front of them and there is not much to do besides party. I was astonished the last time I was home and drove past my old conservative high school. Most of the kids outside looked like grungy pot smokers. (Don't take offense to the terminology- I was one too.)

Recently a girlfriend of mine said something that really struck a deep place of sadness within me. I had teased her about her partying (which consists of drinking and smoking, not drugs) and she said defensively," I'm no different than anyone else my age."

What I've observed is that even people in their early 20's to late 30's have few outlets for self expression except going to the bars on the weekends. I think they look for the magic and excitement that's missing in their lives there or try to hold on to their college days as long as possible.

So I ask myself, "Self, what can be done about this because I will not settle for - It's just the way it is." First off, I'd propose that that is the first belief to let go of. Then I'd say that kids and open minded teachers promote more right-brained, expressive classes like art, drama, sports and choir into the regular curriculum of the schools. Hire more counselors and encourage kids to talk with them on a weekly basis about problems. Hold more weekend events like Snowball (an extremely effective inspiring lock-in thing) so that kids have options besides partying on the weekends. Create classes like "How to Achieve World Peace 101" or "Ending Race Separation" or "How To Save the Planet." Teachers who just give notes and make kids memorize and regurgitate information- Stop it and go take a class on "Teaching Creatively." And school faculty, get over your egos and see that change is inevitable!! Hold weekly assemblies where you bring in inspirational speakers (I'd do it!) or allow kids bands to perform or have relay races like in grade school. Make school fun and interesting on ALL levels for kids.

And if you expect them to be mentally alert for Algebra and English, provide healthier school lunches or free herbs like Ginko Biloba and vitamins. Offer a nutritional healing course or teach about it in health class. There are so many creative ways to make change fun and if enough people think it's possible- it can happen!!! Or you can wait until things are really hopeless and your teenager is doing heroin and kids are dropping out of school like flies- do I need to go on??

And as for the young adults old enough to drink, do you really want to meet your future husband or wife in a bar? Go take a class on the weekends of something you've always wanted to do like scuba diving or a nude drawing class, whatever! Go to a bookstore and roam the aisles- you'll be amazed, you can buy a book, eat lunch or have coffee in them nowadays. Have a drug and alcohol free slumber party with your friends on a Friday and play games like "spin the bottle" and "light as a feather, stiff as a board."

The younger generations are criticized for being lazy and destructive, rebellious and unmotivated. But how did we become this way?? Were there just an unusual amount of "bad" kids born at the same time? I don't think so. In my experience of growing up with a pretty normal loving, childhood, I still was affected by my environment. Let's face it, we may have some things easier than our parents, but in other ways much worse. The world is overwhelming and scary and there isn't much hope offered. Kids, young adults, teachers and parents, it's up to ALL of us to change things. Let's stop fighting and passing the blame around and as Nike says "Just Do It." I know it's not easy but it's possible. Think of what can be accomplished when all of our energy is being used together to make this happen. No one has to do it alone. We don't have to be so separate anymore.

The world is crying out in many ways and it is time to listen. Our youth feels hopeless and seeks escape and fulfillment in alcohol, drugs, gangs, sex, materialism and more. Our adults are still suffering from their childhood pains and look for fulfillment in their children, jobs, extra-marital affairs, as well as drugs, sex and materialism. Our earth mother is suffering from the destruction humans are causing her. What we all need to understand is that everyone feels pain and we must stop blaming one another for it. Our circumstances may be different depending on our race, sex, religion or financial status but we all share the common feeling of pain. And we also share the ability to love. I think that what will help join us is when we can all individually face our pains rather than endlessly pass the blame. In our deepest of hearts, all we really want is love and acceptance. If more of us begin to think this way, eventually we can come to forgive ourselves and one another. The beauty of this lies in the fact that we are all human and imperfect. So if you are allowed to be imperfect, then so is your neighbor. To pass judgment on another would be passing judgment on yourself. Since one person does not hold all the answers, then no idea is more valuable than another. Through sharing our individual knowledge, we can combine this energy to make great changes. I know how overwhelming it can feel to think about making a difference in the world. But change actually starts small, within ourselves. If people can begin to one by one heal individually, and connect with their inner-self, it really Can make a difference. I believe we are on this planet to make mistakes, learn, grow and hopefully awaken to ourselves in the process.

OH SAD WORLD
Oh sad world
My pains sometimes seem
so small
in relation to
the starving bellies
the hopeless addicts
the AIDS victims
the ghetto dwellers

I can no longer turn my head
from such darkness
How can my life be fulfilling
when I am aware of their suffering?
These people are blamed
for their violent lives
Have you ever seen an oil spill?
Innocent creatures
drowned
in someone else's deathly mess
Find it in your hearts
to wear another's shoes
wake to another's morning of dread
dream their empty dreams
hold out their cup of charity
Then you will feel compassion
before disgust
for these tortured people

In Manhattan, there is a newspaper known as "Street News" dedicated to the voices of the homeless and impoverished. People sell this newspaper on the subway and on the streets rather than sell drugs or themselves to make a living. Normally, I'd walk past these people guiltily justifying that I could barely feed myself let alone them too. But one afternoon I was bothered by how callous I was becoming and forked over a dollar for a paper. I began to cry after just two minutes of reading. The dose of reality hit me hard even though I see this stuff on the news all the time. It was different reading the words of these people that were filled with anger and suffering. Especially when the contents concerned innocent children. I'm including part of this piece from Mumia Abu-Jamal that has touched and motivated me in so many ways to continue in my own healing and has given me the courage to share it.

"The children.

They are beautiful, and wonderfully bright, children who know in their hearts, that the rich and politically powerful would rather they were never born.

They think, before they are in their tenth year of life, of death, of God, of justice, and of an ever present gnawing hunger.

They visit the city's glittering downtown, where fortunes are traded every day, where they are treated as trash, and bristle.

They pray to God with an intensity only the very young could muster, and wonder why it seems God doesn't hear.

They hear the public, barely disguised expressions of official governmental and class contempt, and wonder why they are so deeply and completely hated. The voices of these young are, at once, as beautiful as they are haunting.

They remind us that the young are perceptive, and acutely sensitive to their environments.

They see their mothers slandered and disrespected, their neighborhoods made into corporate dumping grounds, their schools impoverished, and their hopes diminished.

They are the children of an acute despair.

Can you imagine the energy we could put forth towards life if we didn't have to waste our energy everyday coping? If we could wake up looking forward to our day rather than wanting to pull the blanket right back up over our heads. Life does not have to be this way!! As Jewel so beautifully sings, "No longer lend your strength to that which you wish to be free from." Let us not continue to let life pass us by because the fear of the unknown and daily survival prevents us from making change happen.

Our planet is in the process of a very exciting and hopeful metamorphoses. More and more people are letting go of old value systems and opening up to the spiritual movement that is brewing. People have grown tired of going in circles their entire lives and ending up with regrets and missed opportunities. Children are rebelling more than ever against this old way of

104

being. We as a human race are opening our hearts and minds to change and to a new more fulfilling way of existence. Creating a peaceful world is now considered by many as a realistic goal for our future. Our technology is even reaching a point where it can help set us free if we learn how to be responsible with it. The more people who discover their inner self and purpose in life, can share this new vision inspiring others, until each person has been renewed with a sense of hope and destiny.

Every event that has taken place on this planet in the history of science, religion, war, education and human struggle, fits into a puzzle that more and more people are able to glimpse the bigger picture. What I have learned from our history is that the only battle left to conquer, the only place left to search is within our own emotional depths. Without this search, nothing else can be truly fulfilling, nothing else will break us out of the endless cycle of human suffering.

Once I began to tap into my inner self, I felt free from much of what had enslaved me for so long. Being able to find fulfillment within myself, I looked outside much less. No longer do I feel prisoner to constant self-doubt, guilt, denial, anger, envy or bitterness. Once many dark layers were peeled off my soul, I was exposed to a life that is truly fulfilling! If these emotions no longer inhibit, what will prevent us from loving the world as a children do? No longer will we feel the pressure of time, no longer will we feel the pressure to compete, no longer will we need to control others. Our only duty in life will be to remain true to ourselves and our destiny. My own walls prevented me from knowing these things for so long. The inner person I have rediscovered has brought great joy and purpose to my life again.

AMERICA
Black woman
I admire your deep soul
The hardships you've endured

the patience you hold
Native American
by you I'm intrigued
You knew years ago
what white man
is just beginning to see
Spanish man
I see the strength in your hands
The hard work you've done
and still a prisoner
in your own lands
America look
at the melting pot we've become
Learn from your people
Stop pointing your ignorant gun
This land is called free
yet so many still feel caged
We separate one another
We lash out enraged
If you look through your child eyes
you'll see we're all the same
Unlearn what has been taught
time and time again
Love yourself enough
to learn from every person
Know that everyone holds a valuable lesson
And one day
when our walls come falling down
We can truly know peace
and turn the world around.

Herman Hesse described "every phenomenon on earth as an image, saying that all images are open gates through which the soul can enter the inner world when it is ready. Here you and I and everything else are all one. Every person comes to such an open gate at some time in life, but few go through the gate or give up the pretty illusions on this side for what we may sense lies within the reality of the inner." Reading this book is one of the gates you have come to in your life. If you listen to your body and how it has reacted to my words, words of experiences that expose my soul to you, you will know that this book speaks truth. Please don't put this away on your dusty bookshelf and forget what I have said. Within you is a being filled with beauty and power and once you believe this, you can help another to see the same within themselves. This chain of love will spread until every human being on this planet will love themselves enough to teach this to every newborn child. As Mahatma Gandhii once said, "My optimism rests on my belief in the infinite possibilities of the individual to develop nonviolence. The more you develop it in your own being, the more infectious it becomes till it overwhelms your surroundings and by-and-by might oversweep the world."

I shared with you some of my deepest personal struggles so that you might be able to find light where you have been unable to see it before. Every mistake, every painful experience, every wall that you come to, is an opportunity for change. The challenge is in facing the reality of your situation and your fear of change. And then trusting your inner-self to guide you through.

Once I began discovering who I really was, I found that one of the things I'd like to accomplish here on Earth is sharing what I have learned with as many people who will listen. I don't really know what the future holds, but that is what will keep life fresh and exciting…just like it was as a child.

So if the sound of world peace bores you, look at it this way, it is going to take quite some time to undo everything we have been conditioned to do for so long in order to restore peace. Chaos before order. So enjoy confronting all of those fears and jump into the unknown. Spend the rest of your life on an ever-changing journey. What could be less boring than that??

Reflections are deceiving
The face in the mirror hides
more than we can see
Behind it lies a vast world
that has been long forgotten
There a distant flute plays
to a sunset of flaming colors
dancing in the sky
Reflected in waters so clear
their depth is unknown
while bodies in their naked splendor
swim
In a world so sweet
it will make you cry
to the new moon
smiling sideways in the sky
its soft white light
showering the lands in a magic
silverdust
Where natures sounds embrace you
chanting
like a secret language
only you can understand
If
you will hear it
in the far corners of your mind.

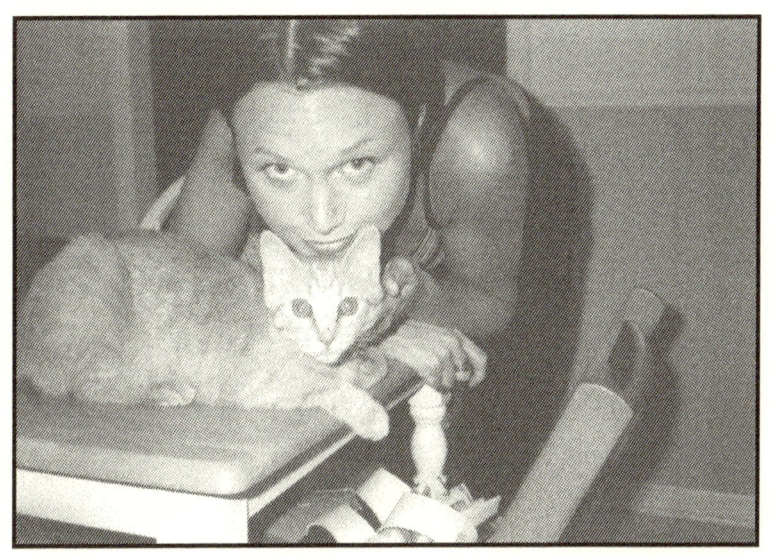

ENVISIONING THE FUTURE

Imagine... a world where people aren't afraid to communicate freely, where your deepest darkest thoughts aren't prisoners to your soul. Feelings are expressed instead of denied or stuffed and there is less fear of judgment because of your honesty. We would tell our bosses when they were being unfair and offer a solution instead of unproductively complaining to our co-workers. Our bosses would listen openly without letting the criticism affect their ego so that a compromise could be made. We would reach out and hug someone without fearing rejection. Lies and secrets would surface from their hidden depths and would be exposed to deal with and heal them.

In this world, people would be given the credit they deserve. We would appreciate the people who pick up the trash in our parks and streets, critics would no longer belittle someone else's work and we would return a smile from a stranger without wearily looking down at the ground. There would be respect and appreciation for our elders advice but we would still make our own decisions trusting our instincts.

The governments and religions of this world would not monopolize people's minds. Countries would be run truly for the good of all people because people will have united and compromised on what was fair for all. And the people will know and understand this because they will be integrated with the inner person who governs their own conscience. We will be able to think and decide for ourselves because we will love ourselves enough to trust our own instincts.

This beautiful world will not be perfect because this is an unattainable ideal. People will make mistakes, occasionally tell lies or hurt another's feelings but we will not be too proud to say I'm sorry or admit when we realize we are wrong. And if there are still criminals among us we will spend the time to rehabilitate and heal them. And since we are all flawed, we will find it in our hearts to try and understand why the crimes were committed and find forgiveness. Material things will never come before the ones we love. And anytime a judgment left our lips we would be aware that we had just passed judgment on ourselves. We would also be aware of everything we said and how it affected others, whether positively or negatively.

People in this world would still be proud of their ethnicity and culture, but we would have an understanding of every other persons background. Children would be taught these differences and similarities about people at a very early age to prevent discrimination when they are older. We would be able to live and work together peacefully because of this understanding. No person would be valued any less than another.

Issues in this world would not be seen in black and white because we will understand that life has many shades and levels of understanding. Everyone would be entitled to their own opinion and every suggestion would be of value because each individual has their own truth. So instead of wasting energy in debate and argument, we would discuss issues, set aside our ego and find ways to satisfy everyone involved.

People of this world will be following their own true desires and not enslaved to someone else's wishes or demands. When people's driving force is love and not need, competition will be a sport and not war. Greed will no longer need to be people's motivation because they will be fulfilled in healthy ways. All dark driving forces such as greed, jealousy, anger and envy will be released through communication so that they cannot nest in a person's soul and drive them to hurt others.

No one in this world will be homeless or starving because we will care too much about one another to ever let a stomach go hungry. Food and shelter would be available to all. Money will be valued less because people will understand that it alone does not bring true fulfillment and will no longer hoard it among a small few. Taxes will no longer feed war and weapons because love and peace will prevail.

112

The people of this world will truly care about our Mother Earth. Every single person will play their part in caring for our planet. Industries and large corporations will spend the needed amount to safely operate without polluting. Since money is of less concern, greed will no longer cloud their minds. People will return to the power of nature and never underestimate her importance. We will seek guidance, healing and understanding in her forests and she will share these fruits with us because we are no longer destroying her.

The people of this world will be free. They will be expressing themselves, following their own destinies and truly living life. They will laugh when they want to laugh, cry when they want to cry, do cartwheels down the street if they want to and love like they have never loved before. This is the world I envision.

BIBLIOGRAPHY

Abu-Jamal, Mumia. "Babylon Basement." Street News. 3rd
Issue 1996: 11.

Adato, Allison. "The Secret Lives of Teens." Life. March 1999:
39.

Blum, Ralph and Loughan, Susan. The Healing Runes. New
York: St. Martin's Press, 1995.

Jones, Laurie Beth. Jesus CEO. New York: Hyperion, 1995

Moore, Thomas. Care of the Soul. New York: Harper Collins,
1994.

Dr. Seuss. Oh the Places You'll Go! New York: Random House,
1990.

SUGGESTED READING (Most of these are available in tape form too.)

The Celestine Prophecy- James Redfield
Chicken Soup for the Teenage Soul (And any other books)- Jack Canfield, Mark Victor Hansen, Kimberly Kirberger
Care of the Soul- Thomas Moore
Conversations With God I, II & III- Neale Donald Walsch
Simplify Your Life- Elaine St. James
Creative Visualization- Shakti Gawain
The Healing Runes- Ralph Blum
No Acting Please- Eric Morris
On Becoming a Person- Carl R. Rogers
The Artist's Way- Julia Cameron
Aphrodite's Daughters- Jalaja Bonheim
The Life You Were Born To Live- Dan Millman
A Woman's Worth- Marianne Williamson
Transforming Childhood- Stephon Kaplan-Williams
Seat of the Soul- Gary Zukav
Jesus CEO- Laurie Beth Jones
The Pleiadian Workbook- Amorah Quan Yin
Bringers of the Dawn- Barbara Marciniak
Emmanuel's Book- Pat Rodegast
Our Journey Home I, II & III- Sage

Please E-mail me with comments, feedback and your stories too at weR1heart@aol.com

About the Author

After reading this book, I hope you will feel like you know me, like I am a friend giving you loving advice. But let me introduce myself with this- I am just like you, a human being trying to find her way through this crazy world.

During a very difficult time of my life, when I was trying to find ways besides alcohol and drugs to cope with adolescence, I began keeping journals to help me try to make sense of my life. What unfolded was an incredible healing process, and a book that changed my life forever.

I feel so blessed to have been able to find my way out of the reckless life I was living which included clubbing and partying regularly, and the sex, alcohol and drugs that went along with this lifestyle. But a part of me, the part that feels connected to others and the world around me, still felt a sense of anguish for other young people. So many of my friends, and youth in general, seek happiness and freedom through this "alternative" life. They seem to be lost without a sense of direction, meaning or hope.

In today's world we are so influenced by a TV and media who have little conscience about the messages they are sending to kids. We drink in the violence, the meaningless sex and dramas portrayed and begin to shape our personal worlds around these images. And then we are criticized and blamed for our addictions and rebellion by the very people who created us. Most of us don't really want to be so screwed up but we don't know how we got to be that way or how to change.

I share my own journey with you now, to offer hope to those who feel they have lost it. Also I will share some insight about life and healing that I discovered along the way. I am not a psychologist or an English major, or even a college graduate for that matter. As I said, I am just a person telling my story. So I open the pages of my soul, in hopes that you will walk away changed too.

www.ingramcontent.com/pod-product-compliance
Lightning Source LLC
Chambersburg PA
CBHW020530290526
45786CB00002B/816